MY
FAVORITE
MATCH

Also by Jon Robinson

Rumble Road: Untold Stories from Outside the Ring

MY
FAVORITE
MATCH

WWE Superstars Tell the Stories

of Their Most Memorable Matches

JON ROBINSON

GALLERY BOOKS

NEW YORK LONDON TORONTO SYDNEY NEW DELHI

Manufactured in the United States of America

10 9 8 7 6 5 4 3

Library of Congress Cataloging-in-Publication Data

Robinson, Jon.
  My favorite match / Jon Robinson.
     p.   cm
  1. Wrestling matches. 2. Wrestlers. I. World Wrestling Entertainment, Inc.
  II. Title. III. Title: My favorite match.
     GV1196.25.R65 2012
     796.812—dc23

                                               2011045054

ISBN 978-1-4516-3176-0
ISBN 978-1-4516-3177-7 (ebook)

*For all the WWE Superstars who put their bodies on the line
and to all the fans who cheer them along the way . . .*

Contents

CONTENTS

A match Steamboat finally sees as the groundbreaking masterpiece I fell for as a fourteen-year-old who wanted to be the next "Dragon."

But that's the thing about a phrase like "favorite match." It's not about the greatest match in their careers or the time they won their first title, it's about the moments that stand out, as they think back on their careers, and make them smile. Sometimes it's the same smile they had when they left the ring—face full of blood, sweat, and/or mysterious green mist—to the roars of thousands. Sometimes it's the smile they tried so hard to hide when anything and everything seemed to go so wrong (like when the ring announcer was accidentally injured in their struggle). And sometimes it's the smile only the showmen themselves share with each other as brothers in battle with one goal in mind: to do whatever it takes to put on the best show possible, even if it means landing on a few thousand thumbtacks along the way.

These are their stories, straight from the Superstars who performed some of the most memorable matches in WWE history. From the time Goldust ran over "Rowdy" Roddy Piper in his gold Cadillac to the time Randy Orton battled Mick Foley with a barbed-wire bat named Barbie, these are those special (sometimes savage) moments, captured in the wrestlers' own words.

Jon Robinson

Introduction

My favorite match? That's easy: Ricky "The Dragon" Steamboat versus Randy "Macho Man" Savage at *Wrestle-Mania III*. I was fourteen years old when I saw Steamboat and Savage trade shots at a mind-blowing pace. Every move seemed like it was going to be the last, with near-fall after near-fall. I had never seen anything like it before. I had never been so captivated by any sporting event in my life. It's the match that flipped the switch inside of me from fan to superfan. It's the match that made me grasp how important storytelling was, not only leading up to the match, but between the ropes. And it's the match that made me realize that on any given night, even when the main event is Hulk Hogan versus Andre the Giant, a sensational story paired up with an electrifying display of athleticism can steal the show, even when that show is *WrestleMania*.

But that's just my personal favorite. Funny thing is, Ricky Steamboat never saw the match as being one of his personal favorites until recently. Until hearing from passionate fans like myself for over twenty years (some of the same fans who sent Steamboat get-well cards and called hospitals in search of updates on the wrestler's "crushed" larynx) finally convinced him to take a step back and have a second look at his match against Savage.

1

THE MIZ

The Match: The Miz versus John Cena
WrestleMania XXVII

April 3, 2011
Georgia Dome
Atlanta, Georgia

I'm standing backstage waiting for The Rock to rip me a new one, and I can't wait. We're building up to *WrestleMania XXVII*, and The Rock has just made his return to *Raw*. I didn't even know what The Rock's involvement at *WrestleMania* was going to be at this point, I just knew that somehow, some way, he was going to now be involved in my match, and I loved it. You see, for years, one of my favorite things about WWE was watching The Rock get on the mic and tear into an opponent. He always had the best lines. He always came up with some creative way to get the crowd cracking up as he ridiculed his rival in a way no other performer could match. So there I was, wondering what The Rock would say about me. How would he get the fans fired up in a way only he could?

Then he said it. "You suck!" Really? *Really?* I remember when he first started talking, I couldn't even believe he was talking about me. I was like, "Oh man, The Rock just said my name. How cool is that?" But then it sank in. "You suck!" That's it? After years of dreaming about this moment, that's all the Great One had to say? I couldn't believe it. I had wanted to be a WWE Superstar because of The Rock. I dreamed of the day he'd get in the ring, grab a microphone, and say something about me that fans would remember for years. But all he said was I suck. That's all he had. I couldn't believe it.

So the next week I came out on *Raw* and I said, "That's it? That's all you could come up with? 'You suck'? Really? 'You suck'? Well, you really got me there." What's cool about The Rock, though, is that even during the weeks when he wasn't performing he would call me. He would tell me, "Hey Miz, you're really doing a great job out there." And honestly, this really meant a lot to me because I thought I was getting lost in the shuffle out there. I was the WWE Champion, but all anyone could seem to talk about was John Cena and The Rock. I was trying to make my way up in WWE and be seen as someone to be reckoned with, but the way I was seeing it, I was lost in the shuffle. I was thinking, "This can't happen. I'm the WWE Champion. I'm the person people are supposed to be talking about." But with two big icons like that, two of the biggest icons in WWE history, it's hard to compete in the eyes of the fans. I think it really took a while in order for me to get credibility with the fans, but WWE kept building me and building me and building me, and that really helped make me. In the beginning, though, I was really losing my mind. I didn't know what the hell was going on, and the more people talked about Cena and The Rock, the more I was losing it. But then Rock would call me up and tell me how I was on point every time I was going out there, and he told me to keep it up. He told me I needed to be on point from now on in order to get to where I wanted to be, and that's exactly what happened when we finally had the moment where the three of us all got in the ring at the same time. There we were, The Miz, John Cena, and The Rock all in the ring. I'm in the ring with two of the best talkers, two of the biggest icons WWE has ever seen, and I'm stepping up to them and really digging in and going at it . . . and I'm shining. That's what made me realize where I was in my career. I was so worried about getting lost in the shuffle when the feud began, but once all three of us got in the ring, it finally became all about me.

The moment I liked the most throughout the feud, though, has to be when I came out dressed as The Rock. That was one of my favorite moments of all time. I remember back in 1999, back in my high-school years, my friends all loved Stone Cold Steve Austin, but I loved The Rock. I used to imitate him in my living room, and I'd just go off. So when I was told that I was going to imitate The Rock on *Raw*, at first I was excited, but then reality hit and I was like, "Nobody is going to believe this." I'm not as big as The Rock. I don't have tattoos like The Rock. I'm not black. I didn't think I was going to pull this off, but Vince McMahon told me: "The people want to believe that The Rock is here. They want to believe The Rock is here so bad that they'll believe you're The Rock." So I agreed to do it, and I just went out trying to do the best Rock impersonation I possibly could.

The plan was to hit the music and listen for the huge pop from the crowd. Then we were going to wait a little bit, and when I went out Vince told me that there would be a second huge pop. I said, "I don't know about that second huge pop. They're going to know it's not him and think this is stupid." That was my fear. I thought the fans wouldn't even boo. I thought they'd just react with silence because it was so stupid that this guy who looked nothing like The Rock was out there pretending to be him. So I heard the music: "If you smell what The Rock is cooking . . ." and the crowd erupted.

I was like, "Oh my God!" Then I walked out and the crowd erupted again. That's when I started thinking that I was actually pulling it off. Then I stopped at the top of the ramp and I smelled the air, kind of like The Rock always does, and the crowd was going nuts. Then I took off my sunglasses and the crowd popped again. I thought it would take them only about fifteen seconds to know that I wasn't actually The Rock, but the crowd was so enthralled thinking that it was really him that people were going nuts for me. I was not only pulling it off, but the crowd reaction to everything I was doing was just ridiculous. People who were close to the ring and could see my face started to get it, but the people in the back were still going nuts even as I got into the ring. Next thing you know, I hit the Rock Bottom, and it wasn't until I took off my wig that a lot of people first realized that it wasn't The Rock, it was me. That was a really cool moment.

Another one was when I cut a promo on Cena, then I went right into the camera and called out The Rock. It was a moment that said, "I'm not afraid of you, and I'm not afraid of *you* either." Literally, there I was, calling out these two big stars and looking like a million bucks. It's one of those things that really made me look like a legitimate ass kicker and really went a long way in helping establish me in that main event scene.

And it's funny because when I first came to *Raw*, the first person I had to go up against was John Cena. I basically went out there every week and called him out. If people want to know when this storyline for *WrestleMania* first started, it really started back then. It was me coming out with my fedora, my bandanna, and my whole Miz gimmick on full volume. I was calling out Cena every week, and my gimmick was me calling him out even though I knew he wasn't in the building. So every week I'd call him out and every week he wouldn't show up, and when he didn't show up I counted that as a victory. So I'd call him out, he wouldn't show, and I'd be up 1–0. It got up to about 8–0 before Cena finally came out and we had a match. He really came out and ripped into me. It only took him like ten minutes to beat me, and while some people thought it shouldn't have been that way, I'm actually kind of glad that's the way it went down. It set me back to where I needed to be. I realized that I needed to go through wars in order to get to John Cena. So, basically, I got to Cena, then I was sent all the way back down and had to work my way up by going after the United States Championship and then finally winning the championship. And if you remember, I got fired at one point on *Monday Night Raw* and had to come back as the Calgary Kid. And that's where everything really changed for me. My look changed, my attitude changed, everything changed. So I went after the United States Championship, then went on to have a couple of runs with the Unified Tag Team Championships and had my first *WrestleMania* ever with Big Show as Show Miz. I just kept building and building and building and building and building until finally I felt that I was ready to face John Cena once again.

I think the moment where I really believed that I was top-tier talent was when I won Money in the Bank. That was one of the most emotional matches that I've ever had. I was standing on top of the ladder, and the briefcase was dangling right in front of me, and I knew that I was going to be the next WWE Champion. Even though everyone always told me I was never going to make it. Even though everyone thought I would be the first Money in the Bank winner to lose my title shot. It just goes to show why I don't listen to critics and I haven't listened to critics since I debuted in WWE, because they never believed I was going to make it. I proved them wrong, and I will continue to prove them wrong throughout my career. That's why I was so emotional at the top of that ladder. I knew right then that I was next in line. I knew right there that there was belief in my abilities to be the next top-tier talent. But even if you win that WWE Championship, it doesn't automatically mean that you're a main eventer. It means you're good, but it's what you do with that WWE Championship that can bring you above and beyond. And what happened after I won the title is that I went on this media blitz that WWE hasn't seen in a very long time. MTV, *US Weekly*, ESPN, TMZ . . . everyone wanted a piece of me and wanted me to be on shows and do interviews, and I don't think WWE or myself or anybody thought that this much media would come through. But they loved my story. It was the story of a kid who loved WWE and always dreamed of becoming a Superstar and worked his butt off. Coming from a reality show, it took me a long time to prove that I belonged. I got thrown out of locker rooms. I was berated and wasn't accepted by WWE when I first started. People look at reality show stars like they're not going to do anything in their life. Well, I did. I wanted to become WWE Champion and that's exactly what I did. The goal I set out to do, I accomplished ten years later. It was a dream come true for me.

And that dream went to new heights at *WrestleMania XXVII*. When I was walking out to the ring before the match, WWE gave me these awesome bubbles that my friends all call marshmallows. I thought they were great, but all my friends were like, "Dude, Cena had this amazing choir and you got freakin' balloons!" But I thought it was cool. I was just excited to get anything, so I liked them. I still use them to this day for Pay-Per-Views. So I was walking out to "Awesome!" and all the pyro that I never had before, and I was so pumped up because right before I came out they played this long video that showed my story to "Hate Me Now," by Nas and P. Diddy, and it was so incredibly done. I'd never had anything like that produced for me before, so I was ready to go. But the coolest part of my entrance came just after I got to the ring and hoisted the WWE Championship belt into the air. That's when the John Cena video package started to play and the arena went black so nobody could see me. And when I looked to my left, there were seven of my best friends sitting in the front row, chanting and cheering for me. Literally, I was in the ring staring at them and giving them a wink as I showed them the WWE Championship belt. It was like, "Look, we all made it." Those were the guys who were wrestling with me in my living room and coming over to watch *WrestleMania* with me every year. But there we were, they were in the front row and I was in the ring at *WrestleMania* in the main event, and we were doing it together. It was great.

As for the match itself, I wish I could tell fans all the memorable spots that I remember, but the truth is, I don't remember anything from my entrance and winking at my friends on. What people might not realize is that I suffered a concussion during the match that wiped away my memory. Toward the end of the match, right when the first finish with the ten count happened, John Cena tackled me over the barrier and I hit the back of my head on the concrete really hard, and because of that I don't remember anything. I don't remember my match. I don't remember The Rock coming out. I don't remember winning. The only thing I remember is seeing my friends. I know I was coherent during the match, but when I hit my head, I lost all memory of it. So it kind of sucks that my favorite match and my favorite moment is *WrestleMania XXVII* where I go over, and I don't even remember it happening. The thing is, bad guys don't win in the main event at *WrestleMania*, good guys do. Look back at all the *WrestleManias*: A good guy wins the main event almost every single time. I'm one of the only exceptions. So it's a great honor to have, I just wish I could remember it. A lot of people tell me things, my friends and family all like to give me feedback on my match, and they all say that when I hit Alex Riley with the briefcase and then John Cena hit me with the AA, everyone thought it was over. When I kicked out, people said I was a made man right then and there because nobody thought I would kick out of that. That was the moment they all remember about the match, even if I had to watch it on DVD to even know what they were talking about.

But when you tally it all up, I was in the main event of *WrestleMania XXVII*, I won with The Rock's help, The Rock was happy, John Cena was happy, Vince McMahon was happy, and I'm happy when I watch it again. It's just one of those things, when I look at it and I look at myself in that match, I'm like, "Wow, I'm really knocked out." You can tell how bad I was hurt when you watch the match. What's funny is that after the match, Chris Jericho actually texted me and said, "You've been working on your selling, haven't you?" I was like, "Dude, I was really knocked out." And he texted back, "Figures."

2

RANDY ORTON

The Match: Randy Orton versus Mick Foley
WWE *Backlash*

April 18, 2004
Rexall Place
Edmonton, Alberta, Canada

I spit in Mick Foley's face. Actually, I did it a couple of times. I was the "Legend Killer," and that's just what I did. I was disrespecting him. I was part of Evolution at that point, and we all jumped him and Batista power-bombed him through a table onto the concrete floor. I just kept hitting him, spitting on him, and jumping him until it drove him psychotic. It drove Mick Foley so crazy that he turned into Cactus Jack. I have a lot of favorite matches, but no matter how good a match I have, nothing tops this match at *Backlash*. It was one of the hottest angles I have ever been in. When I look back, this match really helped set me up for my first World Heavyweight Championship run. I was the Intercontinental Champion during my feud with Foley, but the match at *Backlash* really gave me the momentum to get into position for that next level, and that's one of the reasons this match is really important to me and my career.

Another reason this match really stands out is because of the violence involved. This was a different time, and in this match we had a burlap sack filled with ten thousand thumbtacks. Mick Foley had been in plenty of matches where he used thumbtacks and he knew what he was in for when he landed on them, and I made the decision about a month out that I was going to land on the thumbtacks during our match. It sounds easy enough, but as the days drew closer to the Pay-Per-View, I actually started losing sleep at night. I'm not bullshitting, I was losing sleep thinking about landing on these thumbtacks. So I went to props and I grabbed one of the thumbtacks that they had sterilized and put in this burlap sack and kept under the ring, and I took one of these thumbtacks home. I laid it on the carpet and stared at it for a second, then I decided to lay back real slow on top of it and see what it felt like. It was awful. That was such a bad idea. So there I was, two or three nights before the Pay-Per-View, getting more and more nervous about what was going to happen in this match.

I ended up getting thrown off the stage, we broke a table somewhere along the way, and Foley dropped an elbow off of the stage and onto me. He had a barbed-wire bat and he cut me open with it. I bled all over the fucking place. I cut his arm up with this 4x8 sheet of plywood. It was like a mattress of barbed wire, and I slammed him on top of that, which was just ridiculous. Then I went for an RKO, but he pushed me off, and when I go for the RKO and someone pushes me off, that's a lot of force flying through the air, and so when I land I slap the mat hard. But in this match, when he shoved me off of the RKO, I actually landed in the thumbtacks. And these things were everywhere. They stuck in my fingers, my elbow, all along my forearm, my back, and the back of my triceps. But I have to say, the ones in my fingertips were the ones that hurt the most. And then, to make matters worse, after I landed on the thumbtacks, I sat up and all of these thumbtacks went into my ass and thigh. I sat up and was like, "Oooh!" I was in shock. It was like a belly flop to the backside, only ten times worse.

The funniest part about this was actually after the match. I remember walking backstage and I was so happy with the match. I had that amazing feeling that only comes after a great match, and I kept thinking, "This is why I do this for a living." There's nothing like that feeling after you deliver a great performance. I was walking backstage loving the moment, smiling ear to ear and just ecstatic, when Chris Jericho walked by and said, "Hey man, great match. How did you get those thumbtacks to stick to your back like that?" I just looked at him, and I think he realized right away by the expression on my face that I really took the bump. I landed on those fucking thumbtacks. I was like, "That was real, bub," and I turned around to show him my back. There was mark after mark after mark because during the match, after I had already landed on the thumbtacks, Foley tried to roll me up for the pin. I had a couple dozen of these thumbtacks sticking in me, so when I rolled back, all of these thumbtacks actually dug in deeper. It hurt so bad that I could barely put my back to the mat, so I rolled out of the ring at that point and asked Ric Flair to start pulling them out of my skin. It's actually on the DVD: me rolling out of the ring and Ric Flair pulling all of these thumbtacks out of my body.

Eventually, we got most of them out, then I beat Mick with an RKO onto the barbed-wire bat. We named the bat Barbie, and she ended up coming in handy. And that's the thing with this match: It started big, then it just kept getting bigger and better, and better and better, and the finish was just perfect. It was the most perfect motion when I hit the RKO and that crowd was just into it the entire time. It was the best crowd I've ever had the pleasure of working in front of.

And I remember after the match, I saw Mick and we were both full of blood and spit and tears . . . we were just a mess, but we gave each other a big old hug, then it was off to the car so we could get to *Raw* the next day. That's just what we do. And the first thing I did when I got to *Raw* the next day was sit down and watch a tape of the match. They play the matches so guys who are on other brands or who weren't at the show could catch up throughout the day, and I went right to the TV so I could play the match back and see if it played out as well on the screen as I thought it did when I was in the ring. I was so proud of that match as I watched it that day. I still am.

3

JOHN MORRISON

The Match: Johnny Nitro versus Charlie Haas
Monday Night Raw

June 5, 2006
Mellon Arena
Pittsburgh, Pennsylvania

Before John Morrison, I was a man of many names—Johnny Blaze, Johnny Nitro, Johnny Spade—but the WWE Universe really got to know me as Johnny Nitro from the tag team MNM. After the team broke up, I started out as a singles performer, and this match is one of the first times Johnny Nitro was not part of MNM, even though I still had the beautiful Melina as my manager. That's back when we did what I believe is one of the best entrances in the history of wrestling, where she jumps up and does the splits. And right before her skirt flies up and reveals any naughty parts, Johnny Nitro's head pops up and blocks the view with a smile and a wink that just oozes dislike and disdain, because instead of seeing what they want to see underneath Melina's skirt, they see my beautiful face.

Ding-ding-ding! Before the match starts we get our time cut, which is a typical happening in WWE, so I hustle down, we do our entrance, it's phenomenal, and the fans are screaming. Then down comes Charlie Haas, and he's already bummed because we had our time cut, so he's sprinting down to the ring as Lillian Garcia is announcing his entrance. She announces Charlie Haas from wherever he's from, but she doesn't have time to get out of the ring before Charlie is already there. Charlie's entrance is, he runs and hits the ropes, then starts running back and forth. Lillian doesn't know any of this and isn't looking anywhere except down at her clumsy feet, so when Charlie hits the ring, he hits the ropes and bumps Lillian. She flies off the apron in what seems like slow motion, like a giant cow who gets pushed off a table ... *mooooo*, boom! She crashes against the floor and the match starts. As soon as the *ding-ding-ding* happens, all I can hear are these high-pitched noises that sound like a beached dolphin or an orca that can't breathe right, and it's Lillian screaming about her neck and holding her wrist. She's screaming so loud that—even though I'm the heel, I'm the bad guy—when Charlie Haas locks up and takes me down with a headlock takeover, all you hear is "Boo!" Everybody hates Charlie Haas. "What a heel! He just beat up the ring announcer." He turned the crowd with that one bump.

So Lillian is down, and she stays down for like three minutes with her dolphin noises, until finally I have Charlie in a hold and the whole crowd erupts and starts cheering. They're chanting, "Lil-li-an! Lil-li-an!" Then Lillian stands up and the crowd cheers for her heart and determination. She's barely injured, by the way, from any of this. She sprained her wrist, that was it, but she still at one point asks for a stretcher because she thought she had hurt her neck, which wasn't the case. So the whole crowd continues to chant, "Lil-li-an! Lil-li-an!" and Charlie Haas asks me, "What are they saying?" I say, "They're chanting for Lillian, dude, because you knocked her off the apron."

There was actually a funny YouTube clip, where for a while if you searched for "Move Bitch, Get Out the Way," this came up and there was a shot of Charlie knocking

Lillian off the apron over and over again as they rap, "Move bitch, get out the way!" I don't think the video is still up, but it was quite apropos.

So anyway, Charlie starts to set up for his big come-back—clothesline, punch, clothesline—but the crowd is totally booing him for his comeback because of what he did to Lillian. I hit him with one of my better 450-Monkeyflip bumps and the crowd pops for it, then Melina gets into the ring and pretends to injure her ankle. So the referee is distracted and Charlie is distracted, which gives me time to roll him up. I think that is the perfect ending to this match because it had a real injury. You had Charlie, the babyface getting booed, then you had a fake injury that helped Johnny Nitro get the victory. So it's kind of like this big circle of unpredictability that can only happen on live TV.

4

SHAWN MICHAELS

**The Match: Shawn Michaels
versus Undertaker**
WrestleMania XXVI

March 28, 2010
University of Phoenix Stadium
Glendale, Arizona

I've been really fortunate to be a part of some really special matches, but my favorite match, my most memorable match, was never even supposed to happen.

You see, we were coming off of *WrestleMania XXV*, and I was taking the summer off anyway, and then halfway through the summer I got a call from Michael Hayes and he said, "Hey, I've got this crazy idea. You talked about next year being your last, and we've never really done a return match at *WrestleMania*, so what do you think of doing a return match of you and 'Taker at *WrestleMania*? If you're really serious about leaving, put your career on the line."

I said, "Sounds great," and I heard that we were going to start to build to that after *SummerSlam*. But then I got a call about a month or so before I come back and it was Hunter, and he told me that we were getting DX back together. So the Undertaker match was put on the back burner and we came back with the DX stuff. Not too long after I was back working, Vince had a meeting with a few of us, including myself, 'Taker, and Hunter, and he told us how we needed to start building up these younger guys. That's when Vince laid out his plans. He said, "Hunter, you're going to work with Sheamus and start building him. Shawn, you're going to work with Miz and start building him. And 'Taker, you're going to work with Drew McIntyre and start building him." We all said, "Okay," but we didn't really know how that would all work out. On a big-match scale at *WrestleMania*, all of these guys were relative newcomers at that time, and we were looking at having about eight months for the company to build those guys and have them ready to work with us at *WrestleMania*. But in about November, Vince called me in and said, "Look, there's no way those guys are going to be ready. None of those guys are going to be sellable for *WrestleMania*. I want to go with a rematch between you and Undertaker." I thought that sounded great, and Vince told Undertaker the same thing, and he thought it was a great idea as well. Then he told Hunter and Hunter was like, "What a rip-off." Obviously, Sheamus turned out to be great, and he was ready for his moment at *WrestleMania*, but back then the other two just weren't quite there yet.

After we made the decision, a few weeks later the Slammys were coming up, but now some people in the back were going back and forth about whether or not the rematch between me and 'Taker was the right choice for *WrestleMania*. So I told Vince that if I was winning the Slammy for Match of the Year with Undertaker for our match the year before, that's when I should go out and issue the challenge for the rematch. But Vince was really wavering about it at this point and wasn't sure. So I figured if I just went out there and made the challenge, then we had to do it, right? Somebody had to pull the trigger. So I told Vince that after I accepted my award, I was going to cut a promo on 'Taker. After I said that, Vince was like, "All right, I guess we're going there now."

I told him, "I won't do it if you don't want to, but if we're going to do this, we need to start now," and he was on board. So I went out, got my award, and cut the promo that planted the seed for the match.

Then we all started thinking about how we could make it different from last year. We hadn't determined whether we were truly going to put my career on the line. That was a decision that only I could make, and I told them, "Look, I'm ready to do that." We had a few backup scenarios, just in case I was going to be the typical wavering wrestler and wanted to come back after losing the match, but I didn't want to put my career on the line unless I was truly ready to walk away. I didn't want to kill that retirement stipulation. I wanted to give that stipulation some credibility, and to do that, you really have to be certain that you're walking away, otherwise you're really killing that stipulation for future use. But I told them I was ready to do that and I was firm in my belief that I was not coming back.

So we had the storyline all set: I was going to call out 'Taker, he was going to refuse and blow me off, that was going to set me off, then one of the things that was going to sell this match as different from last year was to have the Heartbreak Kid obsessed to the point where I put my career on the line. I was obsessed with ending The Streak and was willing to do anything to accomplish this. So when we were doing the DX stuff, I was out there making really bad decisions on the air and Hunter was trying to talk me off the ledge so to speak. And the thing is, Undertaker was the world champion at the time, and one way I could get to him was by winning the *Royal Rumble*. Then if I beat him at *WrestleMania*, not only would I end The Streak, I'd take the title. Obviously, in the *Rumble*, that didn't work out. I blew it and I snapped again. Really, my chances were blown and there was no way I could face him. Then we head into the Elimination Chamber, and HBK knew that there was no way I could face 'Taker if he was still the world champion at *WrestleMania*. So that's when we came up with me coming out from underneath the chamber and costing him the World Heavyweight Championship. That put the Undertaker into position to call me out, and he finally said that the only way he'd do this is if I put my career on the line. HBK was backed into a corner and acted irrationally, accepting the challenge and putting his career on the line because that was the only way he would get the match. That's what set the stage heading into *'Mania*.

I remember once we got to town for my final show, that whole day, that whole week . . . It's one thing to think about it all creatively, because creatively, none of it is really real. You can go out on TV and say you're going to kill somebody, but you don't really do it. But this was something that, like a lot of things that I've done, it's where reality and TV sort of mix together. And you don't have to act when that's the case. It's all very real. It's all very natural. So ever since that promo where I put my career on the line, I knew that this was really going to happen. I really just went ahead and made the decision to walk away from the one thing that I've done the majority of my life. That's a different feel. The thing is, to everybody else, this is the storyline. But to me, knowing the reality of it, it's real. This isn't just a storyline. Even today, people still think I'm coming back. They think I'll wrestle again. They can't come to grips with the fact that Shawn Hickenbottom has made a real-life decision that *WrestleMania* was my last match. When you're the only guy knowing that, you're basically walking around by yourself, even when you're in an arena of seventy thousand people. So everything from that day, that week, it was all very different for me. This was going to be, at the very least, my last time walking out for the main event of *WrestleMania*. The last time that I was going to walk away from the one goal that I had made a priority for the majority of my life. I was walking away from the idea that, no matter where I was on the card, I always knew everybody would be watching my match if I did what I always said I was going to do: steal the show, be the Showstopper, be Mr. *WrestleMania*. That has nothing to do with ego, that's the reality. And when I was walking out, it was like, "Holy cow, this is my last time doing this." It was very surreal, and it was a pretty heavy fit.

At the same time, it was a liberating feeling to no longer carry what a lot of people don't realize was a burden for me. It's very easy for people to believe that I knew that I could just go out there and have the best match on the card. And fifteen or twenty years ago, that might have been the case. Certainly for the last ten years of my career, that was never the case. I still cut the same promo, but I was never really sure. That was a name, an image that I felt compelled to live up to every time that I walked out there. I knew if I didn't, people would say that I was losing it, and that's something I didn't want to face. So I worked harder. I did everything I could . . . there wasn't a risk I wasn't willing to take, there wasn't anything I wasn't willing to try, there wasn't an envelope I wasn't willing to push. It certainly helped creatively that we were getting much deeper, which I thoroughly enjoyed. We were selling more drama and more intensity. I always called it being artsy-fartsy, but we were starting to do that and I enjoyed that process, but you still have to do it well. You still have to perform at a very high level. You still have to be at the top of your game mentally, physically, and emotionally. That's a hard thing to do consistently on a regular basis. And when you get older, it's a tough thing to do, especially when you're competing against guys who are half your age and who are hungry. So that was a liberating feeling to me, walking out for my last match, because I realized that was the last time I needed to live through this. It was a bittersweet moment the way I was feeling emotionally on the way out.

That's the thing that very few people know about me, and even less are going to believe: Away from the job, I'm probably one of the least confident guys you're going to meet. I know that I have a gift, I get that, but I don't know anybody who has had the ability to have all things come together more consistently and consecutively than I have throughout the years. You can call it luck, I call it God's favor, but it's just one of those things that I was able to fall into a lot of times. There was never a time that I went out there after my comeback in 2002 when I was 100 percent confident that I was going to tear it down. I could be wrong, but to me, greatness comes from never believing that you've ever achieved. To me, greatness comes from always desiring to achieve. Once you feel that you've achieved greatness, I think you suffer. I think your work suffers. I think that's what really kept me going, as I never really truly felt that I had gotten there. I knew that I had to continue to really pour myself into what I was doing to stay there. I'm smart enough to know that everyone is looking for that chink in the armor. It's like standing in front of a firing squad. Everyone is waiting to pull that trigger, and I was aware of that, so I always made sure that I was willing to do stuff that other guys just weren't willing to do. It takes a lot of time, it takes a lot of emotion, and it takes a shitload of hard work, and it's not a fun burden to carry. It sounds like I'm asking for sympathy, but I'm not. I truly felt like I needed to perform that way because if I didn't, the sharks would come in.

And one of the reasons I knew this would be my last match is that it was the first match where I was on edge. Up until that moment, I'd never been in a match where I wasn't relaxed, where I wasn't, for the most part, in control, where I knew where I've been, where I was, and where I was going. This was the first time that ever happened to me. If you go back and watch this match, you'll see that I didn't sweat at all. I was so tight it ain't even funny. I've always been tight before matches, but then once I got in the ring, everything just rolled. But in this match, I was wound up, I was nervous, and while everything seemed to come across great, again, unless you're the guy living it, you don't really get it. I know how my body felt for twenty-six years in this business, and that was diametrically opposed to how I felt that particular night. I was just not how I usually was on the inside. That's honestly what I remember about the match more than anything. It was work that night, and that has never been the case for me before.

The other thing that really stands out to me is the ending. We kicked around a couple of different ideas and we did sort of refer to the Flair match in some respects, but the psychology of HBK and 'Taker was a bit different than HBK and Flair. One was regret, with me idolizing Flair and our friendship and all of those things; while with 'Taker, we were trying to pull a different emotion out of there. We wanted to do something that in a way reflected the character of both guys. One of the things that obviously helped, both the previous match and this one, was Mark, as Undertaker, showing humanity, showing compassion, even if ever so briefly. And that's something that, because he showed it in our first match, we wanted to show it in this one—but we wanted HBK to stay true to his character from back in the day where HBK didn't want to take shit from anybody. HBK wasn't smart enough to realize that he was outskilled or outmatched or outdone, so we went with Undertaker where he couldn't believe he couldn't put me away, respecting the hell out of my career, and almost not wanting to do this. But HBK looks at him and says, "Don't feel sorry for me. If you're going to shoot me, freakin' shoot me!" That was HBK wanting to get beat by the monster, not the man. HBK could handle being beat by the monster, but not the man with compassion, not the man feeling sympathy. I want you pissed off. If you're going to do it, kill me. And that's a lot of stuff you can't say on camera, but we felt the best way to do it was to have Undertaker sort of look at me and start telling me to stay down with the rolling of the eyes, almost regretting having to do this. And HBK is digging down deep, crawling up his body and slapping him in the face and telling him, "Don't you dare. At least show me the respect I deserve and put a bullet in my head and finish me." If you watch, Mark was so phenomenal it's not even funny, because he was looking at me one moment as Mark

Calaway, then I slapped him in the face and Undertaker turned around to finish me. He put me in the Tombstone and jumped like three feet in the air and literally drove me into the mat. I don't know if he's ever jumped that high on a Tombstone before, but it was a great way to finish the match.

When the match was over, it took some time to reflect on what we had just done. The term "great" gets tossed around way too much these days, like the word "love"; and I was fairly certain that what we did was great, but I didn't want to take anyone else's word for it. I needed to see the match again for myself before I felt that I could be happy with it, and I could be happy that that was my last one. Any time you have a sequel, you want to try and outdo the first one, and that's something everyone was worried about heading into this match, but the stipulation definitely helped in this regard. But yeah, after seeing it, I was very happy. There's no regret; I don't wish I could've done better, and while it wasn't phenomenal, I think it did everything we wanted it to do and more. You can't ask for more out of a match than that. For me, I know how I felt internally during that match, and that's something where I won't be able to tell people that I had as much fun as I did during a lot of my previous matches. But I did know because of the way I did feel internally, that that needed to be the last one. And that's important, because originally, if I wanted, when I made the Hall of Fame, I was going to announce that I wanted to do a retirement tour, but I couldn't because of this match. Then we were going to have Undertaker come out and he was going to acknowledge that I could do a retirement tour. We had planned to do that going into the match, so there was still that possibility of me wrestling a few more times. But after the match, as we've done on many occasions, Undertaker and Michael Hayes and I sat in a room, we toasted a shot of Jack Daniel's, and we sat there quiet for a number of minutes. Then Michael Hayes looked over at me and said, "Hey, if you don't want to do that retirement tour, I'll understand, because I don't think anything will top what you guys just did." I sat there for a minute, I looked at him and Mark, and I said, "The retirement tour is out. I want this to be my last one." We all just smiled and sat there for another two hours. We didn't say much. We just soaked it all in.

5

GOLDUST

**The Match: Goldust versus
"Rowdy" Roddy Piper**
WrestleMania XII

March 31, 1996
Universal Studios and the Arrowhead Pond
Anaheim, California

My backlot brawl against Roddy Piper was a lot of fun, even if we both hurt like hell for weeks after it was over.

Everything about that match was cool. The setting was Universal Studios in Hollywood. Piper had that O. J. Simpson white Bronco; I had a spray-painted gold Cadillac. I remember the first time I saw that Cadillac, I was like, "What the hell is this? I get a Cadillac that someone spray-painted gold, and he gets a brand-new white Bronco?"

That night was very hard on the body. Bruce Prichard took us both to the hospital after that match, but it was quite the fun time. It's one of those things that you can't believe is happening, even though you're living it. So many crazy things happened during this match, it's still fun to go back and watch on tape. But like I said, after the match it was straight to the hospital. Piper had a broken hand, I had a concussion.

Funny thing about this match is, it was never even supposed to happen. The original story had me feuding with Razor Ramon, but for whatever reason, Razor and the company couldn't come to an agreement, so we replaced him in the match with Piper and only had about a month left to come up with something special. Luckily, Piper was

JON ROBINSON

more than willing to jump into that spot, and the two of us built up the match as much as we could over that last month, with me dressing up in his skirt with his bagpipes and doing all kinds of crazy antics. And the thing is, when I was doing all of the sexual stuff back then, it was shocking to people. If I did that now, it's nothing more than you'd see during a daytime soap opera, but back then, a lot of people weren't prepared for some of the stuff I was doing with the Goldust character. Back then, that was the androgynous Goldust, and he was way before his time. I created the character to push the envelope. The writers would give me an idea, but it was all about the performance. Vince Russo wrote a few of the interviews back then, and I have to say, some of the stuff I read, some of the stuff I performed, led me to believe that he's a pretty sick man, but those interviews really did the trick. Saying some of the things I did in the promos leading up to this match, I was like, "Jesus, I can't believe I just said that." Then those promos go out to the world and people are like, "What a sick son of a bitch this bastard is." The crowd hated me with a passion back then, and for them to see this androgynous character blowing on Roddy Piper's bagpipes, that was pretty sick for the crowd back then, and by the time *WrestleMania* rolled around, the fans were worked into a frenzy and couldn't wait for Roddy Piper to kick my ass. It's funny, though, because people are so much more accepting of people's sexuality that it wouldn't get such a negative reaction if I did the same promos today. But back then, the people hated me to the point of rioting and wanted Piper to tear me up in this backlot brawl.

I remember asking Vince before the match if I could

practice driving my Cadillac because this thing was so big. It was a tank. It was one of those huge, four-door old-school Cadillacs, so I got in it and drove around a couple of the stages they had built, just trying to spin it out and get a feel for how it handled. So we came up with what to do in the match, and the general consensus was that we were going to destroy a bunch of shit. They had some extras set up with food that we could crash into, so we did that, and then when we got the cue to go, I punched the gas in this big, giant, spray-painted gold Cadillac, and I revved the engine as I drove down the aisle, and Piper was there waiting for me with a baseball bat in his hand. He was pounding the bat into his hand, like "C'mon, you son of a bitch!" So I hit the gas and he dropped the bat and picked up a water hose. It was this big fireman's hose, and he was spraying the car and water was going everywhere. Next thing you know, he picked up the bat and came around to my side of the window and cracked the window, glass shattering all over me. Then Piper jumped on the hood and started beating the crap out of the car with the bat. By this time, I was already bleeding from the glass spray, so I crawled out of the car, and he just ripped into me. This was a one-take thing, so he threw me into the catering table and hit me with all kinds of stuff. I tried to get to the car to get away, but he picked up the bat and cracked me over the head with it. I could hear the bat crack, I was bleeding from the hit, then he hit me again. Piper threw me on the hood and hit me on the forehead. I guess he was trying for my nose, but he hit me so hard on the forehead, he actually broke his hand.

I was seeing stars as he was hitting me, then—boom!— he hit me again, and I heard the crack of his hand breaking.

I could barely stand at this point, but what's funny is, I looked over at the extras and they were all cheering for Goldust. Everyone hated Goldust at the time, but these were just extras on the set, and they were cheering for the wrong guy because they didn't know any better. Piper then grabbed me and threw me into this Dumpster that was as hard as a steel wall. There was no give at all.

Finally, I saw an opening as he started to slow down. His hand was hurting, he was bleeding, and as he moved to grab me, I just uppercut his nuts. I hit him so hard in the balls that he dropped instantly to his knees, so then I crawled as fast as I could to the car and slapped that thing into drive. The only problem? He was right in the way. I thought to myself, "Am I going to kill Roddy Piper?" But there was nowhere else for me to go, as there was all this stuff behind me from the mess we made of the lot. So I started going. I clipped his brand-new Bronco that looked like it was fresh from the O. J. scene, and I saw him standing there, and he had that deer-in-the-headlights look. I'm just like, "Please move!" Because I wasn't stopping, but I wasn't doing more than five miles an hour at that point. But he didn't move, and when I hit him, his knees just buckled up on the front of the car. He landed on the hood and I looked right in his eyes and thought, "Oh my God, I just killed Roddy Piper!" I thought he was going to be in a wheelchair at least . . . I just ran him over with a spray-painted gold Cadillac, there was nothing else to think.

So what did I do at that point? I punched it and went faster. He was hanging on to the windshield wipers at this point, and when I turned to the right, he fell off the car and I got the hell out of there. Later on, one of the cameramen told me that when I was driving off, I clipped the Dumpster and the Dumpster started rolling toward a Bentley owned by the president of Universal Studios. So the cameraman with his handheld started running after the Dumpster so it wouldn't destroy the president's Bentley. Luckily the cameraman was able to stop the Dumpster, but by this time Roddy had crawled to his car and was now chasing me, and this set up the chase scene where he sped after me all the way back to the arena. The rest was history. He took my clothes off and I had women's underwear on. That moment right there made Goldust. From that point on, we just ran with it and had a lot of fun.

6

JERRY LAWLER

The Match: Jerry Lawler versus Andy Kaufman

April 5, 1982
Mid-South Coliseum
Memphis, Tennessee

My favorite match of my career was in the early 1980s, and ironically, it was against a guy who wasn't even a wrestler: Andy Kaufman. Andy was a comedian, but he hated to be called a comedian, so let me rephrase that: He was a TV star from a sitcom called *Taxi*, and without a doubt, this was not only the favorite match of my career, it was the biggest match of my career, the most publicized match of my career, and it's even been referred to as one of the most famous wrestling matches of all time. In my opinion, this match changed the course of sports entertainment. It was the first time that wrestling got that type of national publicity. Up until that time, our TV shows were syndicated and regionalized as we were down in Tennessee, but my match with Andy Kaufman in Memphis transcended all of that. It got publicized all over the country and led to us having a confrontation and altercation on the David Letterman show that was listed by *Hollywood Reporter* as one of the Top 80 Moments in the History of Television.

And when I think back, we made the buildup to that match about as personal as it can get. You listen to the things Andy said about me, my hometown, my fans, and you know how personal it was. And the way Andy acted,

JON ROBINSON

nobody knew whether this was all just part of the act or if we were really out to get each other. What happened on the David Letterman show, though, is what will be remembered most about our feud, not necessarily the match itself.

I remember when we were about to go on the Letterman show, Andy and I each met separately with the Letterman people earlier in the day. They told us that we were going to be on for two segments. In the first segment, they wanted us to be antagonistic toward each other, and then in the second segment Dave was going to get Andy to apologize for making fun of wrestling and then he was going to ask me to apologize for hurting Andy's neck, and then Andy was going to get up and sing "What the World Needs Now Is Love." What are you going to do? You're on network TV, you're on the David Letterman show, so you're going to do whatever they wanted. But I knew if we did that, that was going to be the end of the feud between Andy and me. If you bury the feud on national TV, what are you going to do after that?

So we went through the first segment very easily, as we were always antagonistic toward each other, but when we took a commercial break, Andy got up and walked away. He didn't even want to be next to me during the commercial break. Then when we got back for the second segment, what happened just evolved. I had no idea I was going to hit Andy, and he had no idea he was going to get hit. The segment just kept moving along, and we stayed antagonistic throughout the second segment and I never apologized to Andy. Finally, Dave realized that something had gone wrong and we were going on too long, so he was going to try to bring an end to the segment. So Dave

46

said, "Well, we're going to take a break and see what's happening here," and Paul Shaffer started playing the music to go to commercial and I just knew in my mind that this was it. I realized right there that we weren't going to be on the next segment, so I knew I had nothing to lose. When I watch this moment on TV now, it's like an out-of-body experience. I just stood up—and I don't even know what I was thinking—but I stood up, hauled back, and slapped the taste out of Andy's mouth. He fell completely out of the chair and onto the floor, and at that moment I figured that I was either going to get arrested or that they weren't even going to show it on TV. But they showed every bit of it, and then, even after that, they took a long fifteen-minute break trying to get order restored, then they brought me back for another segment to wrap things up.

Andy at first said he wasn't even going to come out for this last segment, then he ended up coming out and doing something totally out of character for him. What a lot of people might not realize is that Andy Kaufman would never utter a curse word. He just didn't swear. Then suddenly he burst out on the scene, started pounding on Dave's desk and cursing like a sailor. I'm amazed that they showed me slapping him, but as he was swearing, now I was really thinking that there was no way they were going to show this. I was looking at Andy like, "What are you doing?" I figured he was killing any chance of us getting on the air. Then Andy grabbed Dave's coffee and he started throwing it everywhere, and as I stood up, security grabbed me and they hustled me out of the building. I didn't see Andy, I didn't see Dave, I was gone. I went straight back to my hotel and I didn't hear from anybody. I thought we blew it. That was at about seven o'clock that night. At eleven thirty I turned on the TV and they showed every bit of it. They even showed Andy's cursing part, but it was even funnier because they didn't bleep it out; they put in the sound of a cuckoo clock instead, so every time Andy swore, all you heard was "Cuckoo, cuckoo." But you could read his lips so plain, it made the episode a classic. In fact, Comedy Central was putting together a show on the funniest moments on TV, and the Letterman people sent them this tape to include in the show. That's how funny it was.

It's amazing because this thing continues to live on more than twenty years after it happened. Then when we were filming the movie about Andy Kaufman's life (*Man on the Moon*) and Jim Carrey was playing Andy, Jim Carrey was so into the method acting aspect of his performance that he was walking around like Andy. Jim Carrey was giving me crap all throughout the filming of this movie, until finally it culminated where Jim Carrey spit in my face. This was unscripted, he just spit in my face, so there was a lot of bad blood between us, as you could imagine.

But I guess he forgot that the last scene we were going to shoot was the Letterman scene, and I slapped Jim Carrey about twice as hard as I ever slapped Andy Kaufman. He got up and said, "Ah man, you really punked me out!" Then he walked over to the director and he said, "I hope you got that on the first take because we can't do that again." When you watch that movie, take a look at how hard I slap Jim Carrey. I got him good, and that was no stunt double.

7

CHRISTIAN

The Match: Christian versus Alberto Del Rio
Extreme Rules

May 1, 2011
St. Pete Times Forum
Tampa, Florida

When I won my first World Heavyweight Championship, it felt to me like fate running its course. I had missed six months due to a torn pectoral, and when I was injured, it really helped put a lot of things in perspective. It helped me realize that everyone's time is limited, especially when it comes to sports and what we do for a living, and it made me feel like there were a few things that were left that I really wanted to accomplish. I feel like I'm a lot closer to the end of my career than the beginning, and in the time I have left I wanted to come back and perform better than I ever have in my career.

So when I came back, the storyline was for me to return, realign with my former partner, Edge, and get revenge on Alberto Del Rio. Alberto was the one who injured me in the first place, and he was having a big *WrestleMania* match against Edge, and since everyone already knew the Edge and Christian history, it seemed like perfect timing, as the two storylines were coming together. When I came back, we even started talking about forming Edge and Christian back up again and making one last run as a tag team. We were both really looking forward to it, but after Edge's match at *WrestleMania*, he got the news that he needed to retire due to a neck injury. It was shocking.

I knew he was having some problems with his neck and that he'd had neck-fusion surgery years ago to help repair the damage, but it resurfaced in a way we didn't expect. He went and had his neck looked at by doctors the day after *WrestleMania*, and after a few days, he got the results back and called me. Just out of the blue he said, "I just can't do this anymore. I have to retire." This was a huge shock, obviously, because one minute you're headlining *WrestleMania* and walking out as the World Heavyweight Champion, and a couple of days later you're told you need to retire.

But that set the stage for my match. Edge had to vacate the title, and they needed to find a new number-one contender to fight Alberto Del Rio for the championship. I won a twenty-man battle royal to get the match, then Edge came out and hugged me and said, "This is your time. If you're going to do it, you're going to do it now."

And what's great is, after I won the battle royal and we finally got to the Pay-Per-View, the match against Alberto Del Rio for the World Heavyweight Championship actually took place in my adopted hometown of Tampa, Florida. I was born in Toronto, Canada, but for the last eleven years I've lived in Tampa. So this was the next best thing. If you're going to win the championship, you want to do it in front of your hometown, or at least the place you've lived for over a decade, because that meant that a lot of my family and friends were in the crowd, so that was exciting. Then to top it off, the match was a Ladder match, which was an advantage for me. I've been in so many Ladder matches throughout the years, and I like to think that I'm one of the guys who helped make the match famous, so I was in my comfort zone there. The trick to Ladder matches is to try not to have any fear. And that's the way I approach all my matches, really. You just have to let things fall into place and realize that things are going to happen that are beyond your control, so you just need to be aware of that. If you go out there and try not to get hurt, that's when you get hurt. You need to go out and live for the moment. During the day of the match, I might climb the ladder and look around and think that it's too high to jump off of. But when you're out there in the heat of battle and the crowd is screaming, you just do what you gotta do and you make that jump.

One of the things I remember most about that night, though, isn't the height of the ladder or any crazy fall. Before I walked out to the ring, I can remember standing there and replaying my entire career in my head until I realized that this was the night I had been waiting for my entire career. Then I walked out and hit a home run and walked out as the World Heavyweight Champion. I went out there and all the chips fell into place. Alberto had Brodus Clay and Ricardo Rodriguez out there with him, but I had Edge with me, and that made the night even more special. When I knocked Alberto over the ropes and onto the floor, the crowd was going crazy, and Edge was out there on the floor and he had tears in his eyes. When I strapped on the title belt and looked at him, I could see the tears in his eyes, and I think that me winning the title meant as much to him as it did to me. I had finally won the big one, and I'll never forget the reaction from the fans and the genuine emotion that they had. My fans have struggled along with me my entire career to get to that pinnacle, and it was this huge release for all of us. I'll always remember that moment, and I'll always be grateful to the fans for the way they reacted. I always believed in my heart that talent would shine through in the end, and I always felt that I had the talent to be the champion. Everything happens for a reason. Edge and I split up and our careers took us on different paths. His took him one way, mine took me another, and that's just the way it goes. I never looked at it like it would never happen. I always thought it would happen. I'm just glad that I stuck it through.

The Miz versus John Cena, *WrestleMania XXVII*

Randy Orton versus Mick Foley, WWE *Backlash* (2004)

Johnny Nitro versus Charlie Haas, *Monday Night Raw*

Shawn Michaels versus Undertaker, *WrestleMania XXVI*

Goldust versus "Rowdy" Roddy Piper, *WrestleMania XII*

Christian versus Alberto Del Rio,
Extreme Rules (2011)

Cody Rhodes and Ted DiBiase
(The Legacy) versus Shawn Michaels
and Triple H (D-Generation X),
SummerSlam (2009)

Dolph Ziggler versus Edge, *Royal Rumble* (2011)

Kofi Kingston, *WrestleMania XXV*

"The World's Strongest Man" Mark Henry versus Undertaker, *WrestleMania 22*

Sheamus versus John Morrison,
King of the Ring Tournament

Wade Barrett versus John Cena,
Hell in a Cell

R-Truth versus
John Cena, *Capitol
Punishment*

Alex Riley versus The Miz, *Capitol Punishment*

Zack Ryder versus Primo, *WWE Superstars*

William Regal versus Chris Jericho,
WWE *Backlash* (2001)

Triple H versus Shawn Michaels,
SummerSlam (2002)

Jack Swagger versus Christian,
WWE *Backlash* (2009)

Rey Mysterio
versus Eddie
Guerrero,
WCW
*Halloween
Havoc*

Ricky "The Dragon" Steamboat
versus Randy "Macho Man"
Savage, *WrestleMania III*

Kane versus Undertaker,
WrestleMania XIV

8

CODY RHODES

The Match: Cody Rhodes and Ted DiBiase (The Legacy) versus Shawn Michaels and Triple H (D-Generation X)
SummerSlam

August 23, 2009
Staples Center
Los Angeles, California

The place where the Legacy/DX feud really kicked off was backstage in an argument between two legends who weren't Shawn or Hunter. It was Michael Hayes and Arn Anderson trying to teach Teddy and myself how to hit somebody in the face with a cowboy boot. They both had dissenting opinions. Michael Hayes wanted me to wrap the cowboy boot around Hunter's head like it was a bullwhip, with me holding on to the boot from the part that goes up your leg. But upon seeing me swing the boot around backstage and completely whiffing, Arn pulled me aside and corrected me and told me to hit him like it was a dress shoe. He wanted me to hold the heel of the boot and smack him with the toe. But when I look back upon it, I think they might have both been wrong, because when I actually took the cowboy boot off of Shawn Michaels's foot and cracked Hunter in the head with it Arn Anderson–style, the sickening sound it made was like two 2x4s hitting each other. It was just scary. I was actually going to keep hitting him with it, but I cracked him so hard with the first one, Hunter went down like a potato sack. And since Hunter is technically my boss, there was a brief moment where I looked at Teddy and there was actual concern for my employment on my face. I was quite worried, but that's where the feud kicked

JON ROBINSON

off. It's pretty dang funny to think of two legends backstage bickering like a couple of old ladies about how to hit somebody with a shoe, but that's how it happened, and that was only the beginning.

The storyline of the feud was a beef The Legacy had with Triple H after Triple H's run against Randy Orton. Once that had been defused at *WrestleMania*, it was time for Teddy and me to gain some legitimacy, and there's no better way to get some legitimacy than with my personal favorite Superstar (even over my own father), Shawn Michaels.

And at first, this wasn't something that we knew would extend across three Pay-Per-Views. For us, it was just an opportunity to see how we could handle the pressure and see if we could hang with the best. We had been very adamant during Randy and Hunter's run that we wanted to be a part of it, and this was now an opportunity to be a part of something different. I'm a very impatient person, and all of the producers and people were always telling me: "Just be patient." And when I look back on the feud now, we were just children, and that was really cool because we didn't act like children, and we certainly didn't wrestle like children. That's something I'm very proud of when I look back on it.

Another thing that sticks out to me about this match is how all of the production costs were sky high for DX's entrance. They had army tanks and a run-in from the Army National Guard, and DX glow sticks sitting in every seat, so the atmosphere was just huge for this match. It was the match that sold the Pay-Per-View. But it almost didn't happen the way DX wanted. Before the show started, Hunter and Shawn were rehearsing their entrance with the tanks.

58

But the rules were that you couldn't have a vehicle in the building with that much gas if you were also going to have pyro. You could only have a limited amount of gasoline. It's actually a law. So here's this tank that looks like it was from World War I and we're all looking at it and everyone thinks it's cool. Hunter was going to ride the cannon like it was his penis, so there was going to be the gratuitous shot of him riding on the tank and it was going to look great, but when they rehearsed it, the tank only went about three feet and then puttered out. It ran out of gas. We were watching from another location in the building and just started laughing. This was supposed to be Shawn's big comeback and it was supposed to be this huge event, and the tank could barely move.

Everyone actually became quite concerned that when we went live, the tank wasn't going to go anywhere. The thing just puttered out so poorly, thank God they rehearsed it so they could work out whatever bugs it had before the show started. But it all worked out great for their actual entrance, as the sold-out crowd was dying to see Shawn Michaels get back in there. They had seen all of these ridiculous videos of him working in a kitchen and they'd seen him come back to the arena, but his return was unsuccessful because we beat him up with that cowboy boot. But it was cool because they came out with the tank and the fans had all the glow sticks and there was just so much production value to their entrance. Then all of a sudden, here we come in our black trunks. I was quite disappointed because our entrance was so boring, but that had to make it sink in even more for the fans how bad Shawn Michaels was going to kick our ass. That's all people screamed at Teddy and me as we walked to the ring. And why not? They had a tank. We had black trunks.

But what people might not realize is that I always wanted to get in the ring with Shawn Michaels. He is my favorite wrestler of all time, and the other favorites I have don't even come close to him. This is a performer who has held my attention throughout countless Pay-Per-Views. There's no question he was my favorite. So when the match started, I was in the ring with Hunter, but then as a change of thought, I went over and bitch-smacked Shawn across the face. It was something that wouldn't hurt anybody, but it would certainly get your attention. Hunter then tagged Shawn, and I heard the referee yell, "Tag!" And I was so fired up that when Hunter tagged him, he turned to me and said, "Do you want him?" And I was so fired up—and you could hear this on TV—but I said, "Yeah, I want him. I've always fucking wanted him!" I don't know why I said that. I was just so pumped that I was going to be in the ring with him. Luckily, I was looking down when I said it, so I don't think the camera caught it, but I meant every bit of it. Yeah, I fucking wanted him. This was intense. I didn't know if this was going to be the only time I ever got in the ring with him, so I was going to make it count. And I was actually a little down on Teddy because he didn't necessarily want to get in there with Shawn Michaels. I couldn't believe it. If you have that opportunity, why wouldn't you want to be the first guy in the ring with him, look him in the eye, and see what you're made of? That was important to me, and I'm glad Teddy didn't feel the same way about it. I don't know, maybe Hunter was his guy, but Shawn was mine.

And while Teddy and I went on to lose the match, for me it's a little different coming out on the losing end of things, as I understand the value of the performance and getting the fans involved. A long time ago, my dad showed me a tape of him winning the heavyweight title from Ric Flair in a steel cage. And he showed me how you could see the shadows move everywhere in the crowd, which means that they all came to their feet for the finish of this match. And that's one thing I enjoyed when I watched our *SummerSlam* match. When Shawn Michaels Superkicked me, I laid out in a bridge for a few moments, and that's something you don't see too often from Superkicks. But I was so excited because people all over the arena had their glow sticks and they were on their feet. That's the first moment I had that was similar to something that happened to my dad. That was the first time I was able to pull off something that was echoed in my childhood. And that's special to me, because you don't always get that crowd reaction. I can honestly say that at *WrestleMania XXVII*, I got a lot of great feedback, and that was certainly the biggest match of my life. But going into the next one I would rather have the people be like they were for my match at *SummerSlam* than they were at *WrestleMania*. I would rather they be on their feet and going ballistic. That's my job. So that night at *SummerSlam*, I did my job.

And this feud against DX really opened my eyes to a lot of things about how things work both backstage and on the stage in WWE. Triple H is really just an entertainment master, and it's weird, but he reminds me so much of my dad. The people like him so much, but he's always willing to put himself in jeopardy in front of them, and they like him even more for that. He did so much to help us in this feud, and he didn't phone it in. But I also learned very quickly that while Shawn Michaels is my hero, he's kind of a jerk. That was fine with me. I learned that when it comes to the future in this business, guys whom I was a fan of or enjoyed or liked, I'm not going to ask how their day is every five seconds if they don't want to talk to me. I think Shawn being a jerk to me backstage worked out because it made for a very real environment inside the ring. And you know what? Shawn Michaels can be a jerk to me all he wants. He's still my favorite, and I stand by that.

I also learned something very important from that feud. Shawn Michaels told me, "Getting over in this business is a full-time job." That sounds like it's just wordplay, but it's not. You literally have to be on your toes every second of every day that you're at work. From the time the flight leaves from your home to the time the flight lands back at your home, you have to be on your toes, because people will try to be sharks and they'll try to prevent the guys from rising who really should rise. It's a very political world, but the cool thing is, it's really a lot more fair than people think. You have to bust your ass and work hard and work hard at entertaining people—not just work hard at the gym, but work at entertaining the crowd. Think about how something is actually going to make people laugh, cry, get so angry that they want to jump out of their seat at you, or be so overjoyed that they fall back in their seats in a heap. That's what I learned from Shawn. People will try to challenge you every minute, and things can change pretty quickly in this business, but it's up to you to win the day.

9

SGT. SLAUGHTER

**The Match: Sgt. Slaughter
versus Pat Patterson**

May 4, 1981
Madison Square Garden
New York, New York

I've wrestled over twelve thousand matches in my career, but when I look back, my favorite is definitely the Alley Fight I had against Pat Patterson in Madison Square Garden. It was one of those matches that Mr. McMahon Sr. put together, but there was no referee. Pat and I had been having this big run around the country, but there was never really a winner in any of our matches. There was always some sort of disqualification or interference, or the referee was getting knocked down, so he decided to have this big match at Madison Square Garden called the Alley Fight. I don't think there had ever been a match like this before where there was no referee, so when we went out there, we really didn't know what to expect. How do you end a match with no referee? Who stops the match? Do we just wrestle until we can't go anymore? We didn't know, so we just went out there and tried to figure it out in the ring.

Pat went out to the ring first, and he was a big fan favorite and hero back then, while I was the archvillain. And since this was an Alley Fight and there were no rules, we could wear whatever we wanted out to the ring. I came out in my fatigues and my combat boots with the steel toes and had my riding crop, my swagger stick, with me, and I had my fists all taped up. Meanwhile Pat had his cowboy boots on and a pair of blue jeans with an "I Love New York" T-shirt and a New York Yankees baseball cap, so the crowd couldn't be any more in love with him. We started the match as soon as I stepped through the ropes: Pat charged me, and the fight was on. It was a really tough match because there was nobody there to stop anything. We just kept going on and on and on. It was a pretty brutal match, and people refer to it still today as the greatest match of all time in Madison Square Garden. It was a pretty good struggle and a pretty rough, tough type of match, and I remember the people being on their feet for the entire fight. Every time Pat would hit me, the people reacted with a roar. He would punch me in the head and I could hear the entire crowd roar all at the same time, and it was quite unusual at the time to hear that big a reaction to every punch and kick.

After we beat each other up and down the ring for a while, I was finally catapulted into the ring post and split my head wide open. There was blood everywhere, but there was no way to stop the match since we didn't have a referee, so we just kept on fighting. We fought on the floor and halfway up the aisle, until Pat took one cowboy boot off and started banging me in the head with it. I was bleeding badly at this point, and when I rolled back into the ring, I saw this towel being thrown in. It was my manager at the time, the Grand Wizard, whom I called the General, and he was so worked up over all the blood that he thought someone was going to get killed if he didn't stop the match. So he ran out and threw in the towel, but this security guard thought he was a fan and grabbed him until finally security realized who he was and let him go. It was chaos at the Garden.

But when I saw him throw in the towel, I tried to wave him off because I still wanted to fight, and when the people saw that, that's what helped catapult me with the WWE fans. That's when the fans realized that Sgt. Slaughter was a tough guy. He didn't want to quit even though he was bleeding half to death, and he wanted nothing to do with throwing in the towel.

And while that was my favorite match, Madison Square Garden was also the scene for my favorite moment in wrestling back when I was feuding with the Iron Sheik. When that feud came along, it was during my second tour of duty with WWE back in 1983. I was out with Vince McMahon Sr. and Vince McMahon Jr., and we were having some drinks at the bar one night and started talking about Sgt. Slaughter—what a great villain he was and how there was nobody else like him—and I said to both of the McMahons, "If you think Sgt. Slaughter is a great villain, you should see him as a hero." Here you had the Iron Sheik from Iran and I was a United States Marine Corps drill instructor. We never really got any revenge with the Ayatollah Khomeini and the Blackhawks going down and the hostage situation and the murder of all the marines at the embassy and all the different things going on with Iran. We never got any payback or revenge, so I said, "Why don't you let me go against the Iron Sheik and get some of that revenge in the ring?"

Vince Jr. loved that idea, but his father said, "No, no, no. You can't ever change Sgt. Slaughter into a hero. He's just too good a villain." But Vince Jr. said to me, "Don't worry, I'll talk to Pops about it. I love the idea."

So a few weeks went by and they finally came to me and said, "Are you ready to go against the Iron Sheik?" And

I couldn't wait. Back then, we were taping some televised matches out in Allentown, Pennsylvania, and we would do three tapings in one night. So the first taping, everybody was still booing me and hating me. The second taping, the Iron Sheik came out and he was booed relentlessly because everybody hated him. And then when the third hour came, they decided to have the Iron Sheik run out and beat up this poor kid named Eddie Gilbert. Gilbert was in a match, and the Iron Sheik ran down and just started beating him down. Sheik had Freddie Blassie as his manager, and they called him the Ayatollah Blassie back then, and they were beating this Gilbert up pretty bad. After he finished beating on him, the Iron Sheik got on the microphone and started hollering about the U.S. and Iran, and then he turned and took a big spit on the mat. And right then, that's when they played the Marine Corps hymn. The crowd went into a silence like, "What's going on here?" Sheik had this dumbfounded look on his face, like he didn't know what was happening, then all of a sudden I came through the curtain. It went from silence to "Yeah! The marines are coming! The marines are coming!" People started going crazy because the cavalry was on its way.

I was coming down the aisle, and Sheik got in my face and I told him, "If you want to fight somebody, I'm the man." He said some things to me and then was pulled away so I could get into the ring and see if Eddie Gilbert was okay. After I checked on him, I grabbed the microphone and I said, "Iron Sheik, the things you've been doing here in the United States are uncalled for. It's time to get some retribution." Then I went in and talked about the one thing I've done every day since I was in the Cub Scouts and the

Boy Scouts and the Marine Corps, and I put my hand over my heart and started doing the Pledge of Allegiance to the flag. Everyone in the crowd stood up and started reciting it with me, and in one night I went from the most hated villain the WWE had ever seen to the biggest hero. It was incredible. And this started a big battle between us all around the country, and just like the Pat Patterson feud, no matter how many times we fought, we just couldn't get a winner. So we ended up back at Madison Square Garden and had something called the Boot Camp match. It was similar to the Alley Fight, only difference was we had a referee, but he was on the outside of the ring. The only time he would come in would be to count a pinfall or ask someone if they wanted to submit, but falls counted on the floor, in the locker room, on the roof, it didn't matter. The ref would follow us anywhere we'd go to see if I wanted to give up from the Camel Clutch or if the Iron Sheik wanted to give up from my Cobra Clutch. So it was really a tough battle.

The Iron Sheik had these curled boots that he always kept something in to add some extra kick to opponents and make them bleed. And throughout our battles, I was always the one bleeding. He never bled. And then finally we ended up in this match at Madison Square Garden, and he tried to hit me with his boot but I ducked and hit him with the Slaughter Cannon and his boot went flying. So finally, I crawled for his boot, he went crawling for it, and he actually got to it first and took another swing. But I ducked, took the boot from him, and whacked him in the head with it, and blood was flying everywhere. I ended up pinning him after that, grabbed an American flag, and did the Pledge of Allegiance. Everyone was on their feet, and it was just an incredible moment, as every fan in the building recited the Pledge with me. It was just one of those moments that you can never imagine, how everyone in Madison Square Garden stood together for the Pledge. Years later, I was on a plane and I met former president Richard Nixon, and he came to me and said, "I want to tell you that when you wrestled the Iron Sheik at Madison Square Garden, my cabinet was with me at my home and we were watching the match on TV. And when the match was over, my whole cabinet and I stood up and did the Pledge of Allegiance with you." That was a great moment right there.

But it's crazy to think that the same guy who inspired the president of the United States to stand up and recite the Pledge of Allegiance would need the help of an armed security team to protect me years later after my character became an Iraqi sympathizer . . . but that's exactly what happened. I had actually missed the first six *WrestleManias* because I had a contract with Hasbro to be in *G.I. Joe: The Movie*, and due to a conflict with the toy company, I couldn't be in both *G.I. Joe* and WWE. Vince McMahon told me, "You can either work here or work there." And I said, "To tell you the truth, Vince, I can always be a wrestler, but not everyone gets to be an all-American hero." So we shook hands and he told me to stay in touch. Then just after *WrestleMania VI* ended, my contract with Hasbro expired and Vince gave me a call. He said, "Sarge, I understand your contract is up with Hasbro. Are you ready to get back to work?" I was like, "Yes sir." So he told me to meet him at his house because he had a big idea.

That night, I told my wife and daughters that Vince was bringing me back in, and they all thought he was going to play off my character in *G.I. Joe* and that I was going to be this all-American hero. But then I go to Vince's the next day and he starts telling me about how Iraq had just invaded Kuwait and they were taking all the gold and causing havoc and how he was thinking of bringing me back to wrestle as an Iraqi sympathizer. He wanted me to side with Iraq and say how strong they were and how the United States of America, this dominant military, can't even stop them. Vince wanted me to do an anti-American Sgt. Slaughter. The more I listened to him, the more I liked it, but then when I got home and told my wife what we wanted to do, she was shocked. She was like, "You're not going to do it, are you? You're going to get killed!" She thought the WWE fans were going to lynch me for this betrayal. But we decided to go for it, and she was right, it was pretty dangerous. There were death threats and bomb threats, and then when I won the championship against the Ultimate Warrior, Jay Strongbow, who was an agent at the time, he came up to me and asked, "Have you talked to your wife or Vince McMahon today?" I was like, "No, what's wrong?" So I immediately called home but the line was busy, so my next call was to Vince. Turns out someone called the WWE office and threatened to kill me, kill Vince, kill our families, blow up our houses, blow up the office, and blow up the studio. Thankfully, Vince got in touch with my wife and she was able to go to her girlfriend's house as a precaution.

Luckily, I used to live on this five-acre piece of property in western Connecticut, and there wasn't even a road sign for my property, just a dirt road, so it was extremely tough to find. But when I finally got home, here's this Winnebago parked near my house and inside were four gentlemen with suits on. The guys introduced themselves as my new security team, then they opened up their coats and showed me that they were packing weapons. They were there to walk the perimeter of my house 24/7, and they said they'd even take my wife to the grocery store if she needed to go. My wife told me, "I'm not going to the grocery store with an armed guard!" It was crazy. These guys were there for six to eight weeks and it helped make me feel more at ease, because back then, when we left home for a road trip, we were gone for thirteen, fourteen matches before coming back home. It got to the point that they asked me to wear a bulletproof vest when I wrestled. It was a pretty rough period, but it just shows the power of this business.

One minute you're a hero, you're an action figure; the next, you make the fans so mad they want to burn down your house. Only in WWE.

10

DOLPH ZIGGLER

The Match: Dolph Ziggler versus Edge
Royal Rumble

January 30, 2011
TD Garden
Boston, Massachusetts

To me, the road to my championship match against Edge at *Royal Rumble* was a little tricky, and it was a journey I think a lot of people never thought I'd be able to make. You see, as much fun as I had back in the day in the Spirit Squad, it was extremely difficult to gain any type of credibility after the group had been broken up. This new era began where it was all about people with actual wrestling and sports backgrounds who would beat people up for months in training, whereas we got beaten up and thrown into a box. So it was time to figure out where I was going. Ever since I was signed to WWE, I wanted to be at every practice because I wanted to get better faster than everyone else. I've always wanted to be better, and I want to be the best one day. So when we got a couple of months off after the Spirit Squad broke up, I immediately went back to where I first started training in Ohio Valley Wrestling. I wasn't required to be there, I just wanted to get better. I just wanted to get more comfortable in the ring, and that's what happened.

But when I first got back on TV, I was just some guy shaking hands backstage and introducing myself, and even then I didn't seem like too credible a character, even though I knew I was on the right track and my matches were starting to speak for themselves. I was an over-the-top, smiley kind of guy with the name Dolph Ziggler. At first the name was weird to me, because in this day and age, everyone wants everything to be very realistic and to know that guys are from a fighting or wrestling background. Then in walks Dolph Ziggler, this guy with a goofy name who is smiling and shaking hands. Then again, I just thought, "Hey, nothing has been easy since I've been here. I can overcome this." I always have a chip on my shoulder anyway, wanting to do better, so the few people laughing at me and laughing at my name made me want to kill it out in the ring even more. I wanted to be entertaining, but at the same time I wanted to get my point across that I can bring it in the ring. I wanted people to know that I'm here to stay this time and that I'm pretty damn good at this. I love to show off in the ring and show people what I can do, especially when it's the same people who never thought a guy with the name Dolph Ziggler could make it. On the flip side, the name Dolph Ziggler is something people remember. So even if you didn't like the name at first, I think it grows on people, and after they see me perform, I think it helps me stand out even that much more. So what started out being a little weird actually ended up playing to my advantage.

But you never really know what's next for you in WWE. Things change every day. One day you're on top of the world, the next day you're back on the bottom. So even if something is mentioned to you or you're told you might get a title shot, it's never a guarantee. This is a cutthroat kind of business, but that's just the way it is. So when I heard I might get a shot at Edge and the title at the *Royal Rumble*, I did my best not to get my hopes up. I had been knocking on the door of the title for quite a while, and believe it or not, I actually traveled on the road with Edge for a few months before that and we became friends. I'm all for learning in the ring, but when you're driving between cities, you have the opportunity to learn from the guys who have been there before. I'm a big fan of learning everything you can from the veterans, and throughout the years being on the road, I've learned a lot from guys like Edge, Christian, Kane, and Tommy Dreamer. Whenever I saw a chance to ride with those guys, I took full advantage and tried to soak in everything they could teach me about the business. I've been very lucky to ride with those guys because they've given me little pointers about my matches and how to improve, so it was really special to me to be able to face Edge for the title because he had helped me so much along the way. Edge has been around a long time and everyone loves him, so for me to have been in the ring with him during one of his last matches just adds even more to the meaning of this match for me.

Leading up to this match we decided that we were going to try and really outdo each other in the ring. We stopped traveling together. We weren't going to be buddies, we were just going to be two guys trying to put on the best match possible. It was exciting for me because I grew up watching him, so for me to actually be built up to become a believable threat to his title, that really meant a lot. Then before the *Royal Rumble*, we were able to face each other a couple of times to help build the chemistry, and it was fun to be out there learning from one of the all-time greats. I really appreciated the opportunity.

And in terms of the storyline, it really played perfectly

because now Vickie Guerrero was in my corner, and I was doing the same thing he was doing years earlier. When she was in his corner a few years back, he was using her in order to enter the title scene and get what he wanted, and now here I was, apparently using the same game plan. She really made the feud that much better, because when she was in the middle of the two of us, it brought back so much history. Then again, you can have all that, but if the matches aren't delivering, then it's over with. I was lucky enough, like I said, to learn and to listen and to have several amazing matches with Edge. I was a hair away from picking up the title at the *Royal Rumble*, and it was awesome to be in that situation.

The thing is, I had talked up a big game, saying how I wanted the spotlight for so long, and now they were giving it to me, so it was up to me to produce. Then maybe about an hour before the Pay-Per-View, we found out we were going on first, and I started to second-guess some things about the match. I started wondering, "Are these fans going to believe that I can actually win the championship out there at some point?" Then about halfway through the match, I started to hear a couple of "Ziggler! Ziggler!" chants. And while I was the bad guy, and you never want to be cheered as a bad guy, it still made me feel good that the people were buying in to the fact that I actually might win this thing. When it's believable that you might actually win, when the fans believe in the match and think that tonight might be a changing of the guard, it just makes the atmosphere that much more electric in the building. Then every move and every counter gets a louder and louder reaction, and as the fans start to believe in you, you start to believe in yourself, and it makes everything about the match that much more realistic.

When the match was over, it was one of only three times in my career where I turned the corner backstage and there were a handful of my bosses standing there and applauding. They told me I did a hell of a job and how everyone else was going to have a hard time following us that night. That's when you break out a big smile, because you know they got it. The toughest critics in the world are the guys in the back because they've seen it all. So when they appreciate it, it makes you feel like you did your job. And when the fans see you out there doing your best and they start chanting for you, it just adds so much credibility to everything you do going forward in the future. In this business, it's all about getting noticed, and that's exactly what my match against Edge did for me. Edge did his best to make me look like a million bucks out there, and I'll always be grateful to him for that.

11

KOFI KINGSTON

The Match: Money in the Bank
WrestleMania XXV

April 5, 2009
Reliant Stadium
Houston, Texas

Growing up, I wanted nothing more than to be a WWE Superstar. So when my friends and I were pretending to be our favorite guys, we would always pretend we were at *WrestleMania*. And while I performed at *WrestleMania* in 2008 in a DVD-only battle royal, I don't really count that as a *WrestleMania* moment. In 2009 when I was in Money in the Bank, that's what I consider my true *WrestleMania* debut. That was where my dream came true. I was no longer *pretending* to be a WWE Superstar. Here I was at *WrestleMania*. I *was* a WWE Superstar.

But this match is also special to me because when you look at my opponents in the ring, there were so many of my mentors in this match. When I first got to development, MVP was the first guy I met. I had driven like twenty-four hours and went straight to the building. It was nighttime, but I just wanted to check everything out. As I went in, I met with Bill DeMott and MVP, and throughout the years MVP would always continue to give me these little bits of knowledge about the business, and we remain pretty good friends. Also in the match was CM Punk. He was another guy who really took me under his wing. He always gave me advice, and even now we ride together. We were tag team champions together, and we had a moment in the Money in the Bank match where he and I looked at each other, looked up at the briefcase, and acknowledged our history. Then we went for the Double Dive, and it was a picture-perfect Double Dive where we both dove out at the same time onto everybody. It was a really cool moment, and I actually have a picture of that moment saved on my computer. I still love to look at that shot. It was a cool moment because we were able to acknowledge where we had been, both on screen and off, as he's one of my best friends on the roster.

The thing about Money in the Bank, though, is that there is a lot of pressure because every match that comes out is always better than the last one. You don't want to be in the group that's in the match that's not as good as the last one. You don't want to be the reason that the match doesn't live up to the hype. The bar has always been raised and expectations are exceeded every time, and we felt we needed to do that. We needed to make this the best Money in the Bank match yet, and I think we did a good job of that. And me, this being my first *WrestleMania*, I think I was the youngest guy in terms of experience in that match. So I definitely felt like I needed to step my game up and let people know that I could hang. I needed to show everyone that I could do things out there that nobody else could do. I needed to stand out, and I think I did just that with my performance.

But when it comes to matches like this, I don't really sit around and think too much about new or innovative ideas. Most of the time, the ideas just come to me about a week or a week and a half before. Everyone has their own way of coming up with things, and we do all sit around occasionally and bounce ideas off of each other, but again, we're all pretty innovative guys. Christian, in particular, is super innovative with the spots he can come up with. When you think about a guy like him, he's been around for so long, and when you watch all of the highlights and the things he has done, you'd be surprised. I think a lot of people take for granted how innovative he is, but Christian is always putting on these five-star matches, and he definitely brought a lot to the table in terms of telling the group what might be different, what might be cool, and what might be innovative.

What I absolutely loved about this Money in the Bank match, though, was the atmosphere. The walkway to the ring was at least a hundred yards long, and once I came out, I remember going to do my thunderclap, but the fireworks didn't work right. I hit one, and then nothing happened for two and three—but this was *WrestleMania*, and nothing was going to bring me down at that point. I was so fired up going down that aisle that what was supposed to be this long walk was over in like three seconds. I don't know how I made it down from the top of the ramp all the way to the bottom so fast, all I know is that I was really, really pumped up. I was so pumped that on the way to the ring, I slapped one of the ladders, and right away, my hand started to sting. It wasn't until after the match that I realized I had really injured my hand and done some damage during my entrance. But when it's *WrestleMania* and you have over eighty thousand people out there going crazy and cheering for you and you see how excited and hyped they are just to be there in the audience, you can feel no pain. It's just an incredible feeling. As everybody knows, *WrestleMania* is the pinnacle of what we do. It's our Super Bowl. It's our Stanley Cup. But it's so much bigger. The fans really get behind everything because they know they are about to see something special. To be out there and to be caught in that moment, it's unbelievable.

And while I mentioned the Double Dive, my other favorite move from the match I took from a Jackie Chan movie. Before the match, I was watching *First Strike*, and they have this whole ladder scene where Jackie Chan fights this entire clan with a ladder and he's doing all of these innovative things, like flipping the ladder up his arm. There's this one point where he slams the ladder down, then he jumps up and kicks through the ladder. I saw him do it, and I was like, "Oh my gosh, I bet I can do that!" The ladders we were using were bigger and heavier than the ones in the movie, but I was still able to pull it off. I dropkicked Fit Finlay right through the ladder, which was pretty cool. I knew that this was something people hadn't seen before in a match, and I knew people would like it because I liked it so much when I saw Jackie Chan do it. There was also this other moment where Mark Henry was adjusting the ladder, but he hadn't opened it yet. I came from around the corner and started climbing it while he was holding it, and that was another thing that hadn't ever been done before. It was something different. It was ninja-esque. Unfortunately, it didn't work out too well when Mark Henry dropped the ladder and caught me, then did the World's Strongest Slam on me on top of the ladder. I know I talked about feeling no pain, but that was one point where if I said I didn't feel anything, I'd be lying.

Other than that, it was just an incredible match. And as

far as being in my first *WrestleMania*, this was the perfect match because there are points where people are doing things in the ring, and I'd be on the outside after taking a big move, and here I was watching *WrestleMania* from right next to the ring. You want to talk about having the best seat in the house! I'm watching myself on the Jumbotron as I'm also watching this awesome match go on just a few feet away. I actually had to snap out of that little moment I was in and get back to the match. But that was a point where I had to think to myself that all of the years and sacrifice and being in developmental and sacrificing in the indies and being away from your family, it was all worth it. It all came together right there in my head, and I definitely took a moment to realize how fortunate I was. I really felt like I had made it at that point. Before, there were a few moments where I had felt that I had gotten to where I wanted to be in this business, but there were still a lot of things left to accomplish. Being at *WrestleMania* was definitely something I wanted to accomplish, and I was glad to see it come to fruition that day.

But man, did I pay for that accomplishment. My adrenaline was pumping so hard from being in my first *Wrestle-Mania* and from the crowd reaction that I really didn't feel too much pain during the match, aside from the jolt of the World's Strongest Slam. It wasn't until after *WrestleMania*, after we got back to the hotel and I got into the shower, that I started to notice all of these little cuts and nicks and bruises. As the hot water rolled down my body, I started to feel the pain in all these places I didn't realize were hurt. I had all of these marks all over my body from hitting the ladder and things like that, and it wasn't until that moment in the shower that the pain started to settle in. It got even worse the next morning when I tried to get out of bed. That's when you realize what you put your body through. It's really pretty amazing how resilient the body is. You don't really know what your body can do until you're in that moment and you're able to go through these painful experiences without any hesitation. The body just gets through it. It's not until afterward that you actually realize how much pain you just put your body through. But I wouldn't trade that experience for anything. I remember walking to the back, and Stephanie McMahon walking up to me and shaking my hand and telling me that I really stood out . . . moments like that just mean so much. I think every time you're in the ring, you have the opportunity to prove yourself and you have that opportunity to move up to that next level, and this Money in the Bank match was the jumping-off point for the rest of my career. It was sink or swim on the biggest stage. I'm just glad I was able to deliver.

12

"ROWDY" RODDY PIPER

**The Match: "Rowdy" Roddy Piper
versus "Adorable" Adrian Adonis**
WrestleMania III

March 29, 1987
Pontiac Silverdome
Pontiac, Michigan

The one match that touched me the most person-
ally was at *WrestleMania III*. It was the first time I retired.
Before that match, whenever I walked to the ring, I never
looked at the people in the crowd. I never looked into their
eyes. I always just looked at my opponent. It's just the way
I did things. You see, the audience can tell if your focus is
on your opponent or if your focus is on the show, and if
your focus is on your opponent it helps everyone get more
into the moment. But at *WrestleMania III*, they had this cart
shaped like a little ring that took you to the real ring, which
was in the middle of the Pontiac Silverdome. They wanted
everyone to take this cart because it was just such a long
way to the ring. I remember waiting for the cart to come
pick me up for my Hair vs. Hair match against Adrian
Adonis, and I was standing there with Vince McMahon
when the cart malfunctioned. Nobody knew what to do,
but in a split second I made the decision to just start running down the aisle. It was a long way, but luckily I was in
pretty good shape back then and I made it just fine. There
were about ninety-three thousand people at the show, and
by the time I got to the ring, ninety-three thousand people
were screaming my name. It's the first time I actually
turned and looked at the people, and it was an amazing

feeling that they were kind enough to give me. It's hard to explain, but there's a chemistry that happens in the middle of the ring when you make a connection with the people, and just knowing how the fans were treating me and what they meant to me and my family, that moment meant more to me than any other moment in my career. It was amazing.

To build up the match between us, Adrian went out and started *The Flower Shop* to oppose *Piper's Pit*. At the time, I think there had been Jesse Ventura's *Body Shop*, Blackjack Mulligan's BBQ Pit, and Jake "The Snake's" *Snake Pit*, so there were other shows out there, but no show tried to rival *Piper's Pit* until then. And then there was Adrian, who would come out in this dress and goofy hat, and he was such a tremendous performer in this dress, weighing in at about three hundred pounds. Adrian is the only guy I know who you could put in a dress, but he's still all guy.

A lot of people don't realize that Adrian and I had a long history together before we ever got to *WrestleMania*. When we were both twenty-two years old, we were actually a tag team out of Los Angeles called The 22s.

We had known each other for about twelve years by the time this angle played out, so our interviews between *The Flower Shop* and *Piper's Pit* really caught everyone's attention. Our chemistry together was just so strong. And then to roll into *WrestleMania III*, it was wonderful to be able to give the fans a performance that they hadn't seen before. I knew with our chemistry, the match was going to be great, so I had that in my back pocket as I took off and ran toward the ring to start the match.

We decided at the last minute to have the loser get his

head shaved. So there was no room for a mistake here, because at the time, I was retiring to go off to Hollywood to go shoot a movie called *They Live*, and if I showed up to the set with my head shaved, that would've changed things considerably. I think that was the first time a wrestler was ever leaving to shoot a major motion picture, so all of that was in the mix heading into the match: our chemistry together, the movie, *The Flower Shop*, Adrian's great performing skills, the biggest indoor crowd for any show in America. You put that all together with the cart breaking down and the people seeing me take off and start running to the ring . . . you can't make this stuff up. It just sparked magic, and when I got into the ring, holy cow! You can't construct a moment like that. You can get close, but wow, was that special.

What was great about wrestling Adrian was that there wasn't much of anything that he couldn't do. When you're a tag team with somebody that young, you get to know them in a way that few others do. And then to have him come back and rival me twelve years later, that's the kind of magic and chemistry that only happens with time and familiarity. There was a lot of history in that ring. There was a lot of hard work and sweat and blood and tears that went into making that match happen. We were so well seasoned at that time and rolling so hard into that moment, the match went pretty smooth until the end. I think the hardest part of that match was actually cutting Adrian's hair. When you try to cut a man's hair and it's wet, it's torture to cut. Luckily for me, Brutus Beefcake came down to the ring for the end of the match. So after I won and it was time to cut Adrian's hair, I just said: "Brutus, you cut his hair." And from then on, he became Brutus "The Barber."

He went through so much turmoil just trying to cut Adrian's hair, he deserved the new nickname. Adrian actually got mad at me for letting Brutus cut his hair because he did such a brutal job. Brutus was excited and thought I was doing him a favor, but really I wasn't. I can still picture Brutus standing there trying to cut the hair, Adrian mad because his hair was getting pulled out, and Adrian's manager at the time, Jimmy Hart, running around and screaming in his high voice, "Piper, *you're* supposed to cut his hair!" You can't plan a moment like that. And that's the thing about our business: For seasoned professionals, it's the stuff that's not planned that makes the magic. You can have a match that's rated a perfect 10, but to me, I love it when something odd happens and you capitalize on it. And when you have a crowd that's really into it and they're showing you the kind of love that they did out in the Silverdome, I could turn around and give them a special performance, and so could Adrian. His timing was impeccable, and that really helped make the match sing.

And then from an emotional standpoint, the way the crowd reacted to everything I did that night, I'll never forget it. It's because of the fans that this is my favorite match. Like I said, that was the first time I really looked out into the crowd and they looked at me, and there was so much chemistry. I remember Jesse Ventura and Gorilla Monsoon were calling the match, and afterward they told me that it was so loud, they couldn't hear each other talk even though they were sitting right next to each other because these people were making so much noise. That was my moment.

13

"THE AMERICAN DREAM"
DUSTY RHODES

**The Match: Dusty Rhodes
versus "Superstar" Billy Graham**

September 26, 1977
Madison Square Garden
New York, New York

This was the first match in our trilogy. At the time, "Superstar" Billy Graham and I built up a tremendous rivalry, and all three matches in the trilogy were great, but the first one was truly outstanding. Out of all the great confrontations I've had, this match with Billy Graham at the Garden is by far my favorite.

This match signified a change in the business. It showed how important the interview could be in building up a feud. In one corner, you had "Superstar" Billy Graham, a guy who looked like a Greek god. In the other corner, you had me, the common man, "The American Dream." We really did such a great job with our promos to build up the match that the Garden not only sold out, but there were celebrities everywhere. Andy Warhol, Cheryl Tiegs, George Steinbrenner . . . The Garden was the place to be, and all of these people came to see the Greek God, the Roman Gladiator, take on the Common Man.

I had actually met Andy Warhol prior to this and we had become friends. The first time I met Andy, he invited me to go to Studio 54 with him, and in my mind, I assumed I'd be standing in line, feeling like a nobody and everything that goes along with that scene. But when Andy showed up, he parted the seas and we walked right in. I was actually there the night Mick Jagger's wife rode the white horse into Studio 54. I was inside the building when that happened. It was just an amazing era to be a part of.

But when I think back to this match, I think back to my childhood in Texas. All you ever heard about was Madison Square Garden, and I couldn't wait to go there. I wanted to see a concert there one day, and little did I know I would end up headlining a show there. That far exceeds anything else I had ever done, ringwise.

To this day I can still remember the roar of the crowd for our entrances. There was nothing piped in. There weren't people out there holding up a card that said "Clap!" Those were real fans screaming their loudest, and it nearly blew the roof off the Garden. It was an amazing moment. When I got to the ring, I could feel the crowd, then I looked out and I could see my mom sitting in the seat I got her. Then I saw Andy Warhol and all of his entourage, who had also been caught up in this unbelievable moment. This was an amazing time for us and our business. Back then, the road went on forever and the party never ended.

I remember throughout this great match, me and "Superstar" Billy Graham were not only entertaining the crowd, we were entertaining each other to the point that neither one of us wanted to leave the ring. Neither one of us wanted to pin the other because we didn't want the match to end. And then when the match did end in a disqualification, we didn't want to leave that moment. I remember looking back at the tape, and I didn't want that moment to end. I didn't want this time in my life to be over. The thing about it is, every match is basic. It's just two guys going into the ring. But it's what you bring to it that makes the difference. It's the excitement, the charismatic impact you have on an audience that makes it special. That's why WWE is so successful. It's the glamour and glitz and everything that goes with it. It's not about the mechanics of the match, it's about everything that surrounds it. That's why some guys never get over with the crowd. They're so concentrated on the mechanics of the match that they forget that wrestling is about these special moments that happen. It's about building up the drama. It's about the moment that surrounds all of this technical stuff that really makes a match special.

But the rage and the thunder of the moment were possible because of the interviews we did leading up to the match. Vince McMahon Jr. had done the interviews, and this was not the usual buildup for a match back then. You had two of the most colorful people in the history of this business going all out in these interviews, and we helped change the landscape of our industry by bringing that type of energy to hyping each match. And sometimes things are hyped so much, maybe too much, and the game can't be played or is a letdown to fans when the match actually happens. But not here. We took the energy from the hype and rode it into the match to elevate our performance even more. "Superstar" Billy Graham versus Dusty Rhodes, that was the birth of a trilogy. And the way the crowd reacted, we could've done more than three, but three was just right. And like I said, this was more than just a match to me. It was about the people involved, the people who came, and the people leaving in the limo with me. There I was, driving through Manhattan, just a kid from Texas going to the Lone Star Café to sit down and eat with Andy Warhol and his friends after the match. This was more than a match, it was a moment.

And, like I said, this moment kept right on going after the match, as the afterparty was actually a party for Omar Sharif, who had also attended our show. I kept looking at this guy, and I was looking at him during the match because I knew he looked familiar, then finally when I was at the restaurant at the afterparty I remembered he was the guy from *Lawrence of Arabia*. It had finally hit me.

I remember the *New York Times* ran an article the next day that talked about Andy Warhol bringing the three-hundred-pound–wrestler "The American Dream" Dusty Rhodes to Omar Sharif's party, and I remember Andy sitting there and talking to me about the match. He told me: "I've never been so entertained in all my life."

14

MARK HENRY

The Match: "The World's Strongest Man"
Mark Henry versus Undertaker
WrestleMania 22

April 2, 2006
Allstate Arena
Rosemont, Illinois

My favorite match is a Casket match, which is funny since I'm claustrophobic. But leading up to the match Undertaker and I had at *WrestleMania 22*, we actually wrestled in the longest match of my career during a house show in Memphis. We worked almost thirty minutes, and it was a challenge for me to put in that much time. I'm not the athlete with the most endurance out there, and most of my matches are only ten to fifteen minutes. Any more than that, more than likely I'm going to get my wig split. But that house show really got us in a good groove and was probably my best performance ever. Too bad only the people in Memphis that night got to see it. But like I said, it really helped set up our match at *WrestleMania*. We went about twenty-two minutes at the Pay-Per-View, and it was a very entertaining match. I fought back from a lot of adversity because I was dieting very hard at the time and I was cramping. I didn't have enough fluids in me, I guess, and I was cramping worse than I ever had before. I remember when I went inside the coffin, my stomach and right oblique started locking up, so I was trying to turn to ease some of the pain, but I couldn't really move because I was in a coffin. It was brutal.

But I really appreciate Undertaker for letting me be a

part of The Streak. What's so impressive about Undertaker's Streak is that, not only has it made his career for eighteen years, but it's helped make his competitors' too.

Nothing can top being in *WrestleMania* and being involved in a match that big against Undertaker. I remember walking out to the ring, and the fans were so loud I couldn't hear anything. And the thing about it is, when I came into the business, I didn't get into it for the adulation of the crowd, but I'm proud to say that I still ended up one of the more popular entities in the business, especially for big men. When people mention big guy wrestlers, they are always going to have to throw my name in the mix, and I take a lot of pride in that. People are always going to mention guys like King Kong Bundy, Bam Bam Bigelow, One Man Gang, Andre the Giant, Big John Studd . . . the bigger guys who have competed for this company over the years, and I think they are going to mention my name with them. Two hundred years from now, my name will still be mentioned with those guys, and I'll be in the dirt by then, but I still take a lot of pride in that. Powerlifter, Olympic strong man, WWE Superstar, two hundred years from now, people will say: "Who is this Mark Henry guy?" And a lot of it will come from being part of Undertaker's Streak.

Working with Undertaker is just an incredible experience. You basically just try your best not to get embarrassed. One thing about working with somebody who is very good is that if you don't step up, you're going to look like shit. And every match that I have with him, I strive to be the guy who doesn't look like shit.

My biggest problem with the *WrestleMania* match, though, was being in that damn coffin. To be in a coffin for five minutes is about five minutes longer than you ever want to be in one. I'm claustrophobic, so there was a lot of me talking to myself and trying to calm myself down when I was inside that coffin. I figured eventually they'd open that thing up, and when I finally saw light again, it was seriously like being reborn. It's hard to put into words how I felt after that match. I watch it again on tape and I'm like, "Damn, that was me in that coffin." When I finally got out, I was so happy, it was like I'd discovered America.

My favorite part of the match was when I had him right where I wanted him, then he flipped the script on me. I was pounding him and pounding him, trying to get him in that damn coffin, but every time I tried to shut the door, he just kept putting his hand up. I ended up giving him a big boot, slamming him over the top and knocking him into the casket. I jumped into the casket with him and just started pounding him in the face, but Undertaker's hand is so strong that he grabbed me and drove me out of the casket. I remember when his hand hit my throat, the whole crowd was so loud that he was talking and saying something to me, and he was within arm's reach, but it was just too loud to hear. It was unbelievably crazy.

15

SHEAMUS

The Match: Sheamus versus John Morrison
King of the Ring Tournament

November 29, 2010
Wells Fargo Center
Philadelphia, Pennsylvania

I've had so many special matches—the Cage match at TLC, the *WrestleMania* match against Triple H— but my favorite is the match where I became King of the Ring against John Morrison. It was a three-hour *Raw*, and the King of the Ring tournament is one of those special things that, as a fan, you always look forward to seeing, so as a WWE Superstar, I couldn't wait to be a part of it.

I had just lost to John Morrison at *Survivor Series* and I had already been beaten by Randy Orton and Triple H beforehand, and I even lost to Santino going in to the tournament. (Let's just erase that from the history books!) But Morrison and I have great chemistry out there. I come out with this physical aggression against his high-flying aerial style, and that combination proves to make for a great contest.

The thing about the match that really stands out to me, though, was the crowd. It was pinfall after pinfall attempt, and the fans were eating it up. They were so into it and re-acting to every big move like it was the last, and they really made it special for us to be out in the ring.

The match against John was actually my second match that night, as I had wrestled Kofi Kingston earlier in the show in order to advance. What fans might not realize is how physically tough it is to wrestle multiple times in one night. Physically, you really need to be on your game, especially with the road schedule we go through on a normal basis. Then to go in and have matches with guys like Kofi and John on the same night can really be grueling. But that's the thing about being in WWE. We're the best athletes out there of any sport. We don't take breaks. We don't have seasons. We don't take time off. We just keep going. That's why you see us come out to the ring in the shape that we're in. If we didn't work on our bodies and make getting in shape a full-time job, we wouldn't be able to have the type of matches that we do.

And when I think back to that match against John, one moment really stands out in my mind and is a great example of what I'm talking about when I mention the kind of shape we are in. John was up on the top rope, and I yanked him off by his arm and put him in a submission right there. It looked like the match was over, but John is such a phenomenal athlete that he can escape from anything, and the crowd really didn't know what to think from that point on or how it was going to end. Next thing you know, John goes for Starship Pain, but I hit him with a Brogue Kick instead and that was it. Look at John Morrison's face now, then look back to pictures before our match. He used to be a lot prettier before I started kicking him in the face.

But the great thing about wrestling John is that we're just two Superstars who not only gel together, but we see the bigger picture of where we want to be. We see Triple H and John Cena and the legends who headline *Wrestle-Mania* and that's where we want to be, and we figured, "Let's get there together by putting on great match after great match." Nobody is going to be around forever, but we want to be remembered, and the only way to be remembered is to go out and do things people haven't seen before. Unless you go out there and give 110 percent, you'll never be remembered, because those legends who have come before us in WWE have already done so much. It's up to us to step up and show that we belong, and that's what we tried to do when we were in the ring. We went out there to do the best match that we could. We wanted to raise our game and take things to the next level. Like I said, if you don't go out there and do something special, you'll never reach that elite status. People pay to see John Cena and Triple H and Randy Orton, but I want them talking about Sheamus. I want them talking about John Morrison. So we went out there with every intent to have fans walk away talking about our match at King of the Ring. We went out there wanting to be noticed.

That's why it's funny when people ask me about how white I am or when I see signs in the crowd comparing me to mayonnaise. Because I look so different, because I can't tan and have orange hair, that makes me stand out, and in WWE, that's exactly what I'm looking for. Sure, if I stand in the sun too long I turn red, then I instantly turn back to white. Sure, I can't tan. But when fans see me, I'm instantly recognizable as the shiny white guy who will kick your head off, and that means more to me than having a great tan ever could.

16

WADE BARRETT

The Match: Wade Barrett versus John Cena
Hell in a Cell

October 3, 2010
American Airlines Center
Dallas, Texas

There were only six days between *NXT* ending and The Nexus attacking *Monday Night Raw* and John Cena. I remember heading to the building that Monday, and all of the guys from *NXT* were called into a private meeting with Vince McMahon and some of the agents, and that's when they told us about the plan that they had for us to go out and not only take out the biggest star of the show, but rip the show completely apart. We were told about it only five hours before it happened, and we weren't allowed to even tell anyone else in the locker room about the plan. They wanted to make sure nobody texted the story out to anyone or told our friends and family, so they basically had us on lockdown in order to keep this big surprise. We weren't expecting it to be quite as impactful as it was, but boy, were we wrong: This was the night that we destroyed the ring and actually tore the ropes down and ripped the canvas back and exposed what was underneath.

We've all seen the ring broken down many times because it's part of paying your dues. When you're in an independent league or in development in WWE, a lot of times it's your job to help break down the ring, so it was no big deal for us to see it that way. But to the fans, this is something they never see, and it made an amazing visual impact on everyone who was watching. The crowd had never seen the ring in that state before, so we were surprised by the type of crowd reaction we got. And obviously, we were very pleased when we got to the back and saw the video feeds of the crowd with their mouths wide open in shock. The crowd knew they had seen something very unique and very powerful, and that was the start of The Nexus right there, going after not only John Cena, but destroying the entire ring and everyone and anything around it.

And what was great about the feud between The Nexus and John Cena was John's attitude toward us. I think he was actually quite impressed with the way we handled ourselves fresh off of *NXT*. We were termed rookies on the show, but the majority of us have had about seven or eight years' experience wrestling. We might not have had that main event level of experience, but most of us have wrestled before, and I think that's what helped separate the Season One *NXT* rookies. And because of that experience, there wasn't that huge a jump for us to make from working *NXT* to working on *Raw*, because WWE has so many agents and so many experienced guys like John Cena, Randy Orton, Chris Jericho, and William Regal who will help you out and give you pointers. And those pointers really go a long way when you're trying to build a name for yourself.

When I look back, I think that a lot of people expected me to crack under the pressure, as one minute I'm on *NXT*, and the next I'm part of the main focal point of *Raw*. That's a huge jump, to go from independent wrestling to a developmental territory to *NXT* to going after the top guy on the show and being involved in an angle that ended up being the main focal point of *WWE Raw* and a few Pay-Per-Views.

To be honest, I just tried to take it all in stride. I knew that this was an opportunity I'd been looking forward to my whole life. This was why I went into wrestling. This was what I'd been working toward for so many years, so I wasn't going to blow it by walking out and acting nervous and blowing my one and only chance to make a name for myself in WWE. People kept coming up to me and complimenting me about how I wasn't feeling the pressure of the situation I was in and how I wasn't showing any nerves. To be honest, I've never felt less pressure on me since I've been in WWE than when The Nexus first premiered. I was a part of the focal point of the show, and that's something I always wanted. I always feel more pressure when I'm not involved in anything or I don't have such a huge storyline. I actually put more pressure on myself when I'm not in such a high-profile storyline, because then the pressure is on me to do something to claw my way back up to the top.

Luckily, that wasn't the case with The Nexus storyline. We had been in the main event at *SummerSlam* in a big fourteen-man tag match, then we had another big match at *Night of Champions*, but my match against John Cena at *Hell in a Cell* was different because it was my first big, high-profile Pay-Per-View match as a singles performer. Everything else we had done up to this point was as a team, so I have to admit, it was a bit nerve-racking to go out there knowing I had to do this match without any help. The crowd absolutely hated me and they absolutely loved John, so it was very black and white, and that's always the ideal way to start a match.

The thing I remember most about this match, however, is just how heavy my body felt the first two minutes. My legs felt like lead, my arms felt like lead, and if you watch the first couple of minutes on DVD, you'll see how slowly I was moving. My body just felt so heavy and I was so nervous, it wasn't until I kicked out for the first time that I really got into the swing of things and my adrenaline started pumping and I started feeling natural again. I've never felt that way before in my career, but there was just so much riding on that match for me and for the company in terms of the amount of business this match pulled in, that my nerves got the best of me when things started. Sometimes you just need that first hit to wake you up.

After that, I really enjoyed the match and the way everything flowed. I think when the match started, the crowd just kept waiting for The Nexus to get involved. I don't think many people thought that I could beat John Cena by myself, so I think the crowd knew the whole time that The Nexus guys were going to run down and try to get involved in the fight. So what I really liked about the match is the fact that we brought them down pretty early. If you look at the duration of the match, I think we brought them down about halfway through, and then they were chased away, so that really left a big question mark with the fans about how things were going to end. Once we took the Nexus guys out of the equation, it really opened up the possibilities for how we could conclude the match.

And I really like how the ending played out between John and me. I hit him with my finisher, the Wasteland, and up until that point, nobody had ever kicked out of it, so when John kicked out the crowd went crazy. Everyone was very, very surprised that he had kicked out. And then he hit me with his Attitude Adjustment, and naturally, everyone thought it was over right there. But then I kicked out and the crowd was in total shock, but that really left the ending wide open where either guy could pull it out, and that really added to the excitement in the arena.

Next thing you know, John locked me in his STF submission move, and that's when we had two guys from the crowd run into the ring. It was Michael McGillicutty and Husky Harris from *NXT* Season Two, and they got involved in the match and helped me win out of nowhere. We had a nice swerve there that people didn't expect to happen, and I think it was a great call to end the match. I remember the fans not really knowing what was going on at first, because sometimes you'll get a fan who is drunk in the crowd and he tries to jump into the ring (which is never a good idea). But we really had a lot of people scratching their heads and wondering what was happening, and in WWE, that's always a good thing. When you can do a finish that the people can't anticipate, and you pull it off in a big moment like this, you know you're doing something right.

17

R-TRUTH

The Match: R-Truth versus John Cena
Capitol Punishment

June 19, 2011
Verizon Center
Washington, D.C.

Throughout my career, all I've ever heard is how I'd never make it to the main event. That's why my match against John Cena at *Capitol Punishment* means so much to me. It's the match where I showed people that I had made it. I did it. There I was against the most popular performer in all of wrestling, and we were in the main event. You can never take that away from me.

And it all started with "Little Jimmy." Vince McMahon gave me the line, how all the John Cena fans were the "Little Jimmys" of the world, and I just took the line and ran with it. There's Little Jimmy, Big Jimmy, and even Mamma Jimmy out there in the crowd, and they're all cheering for Cena, not me. And like I say, you kick my dog, I'll kick your cat, so if you go out and boo me, then I'm going to do whatever it takes for you to hate me even more. And I think the way it's worked out . . . the fans love to hate me. And a lot of that has to do with how fast I turned from the good R-Truth, who was out there rapping for them and shouting "What's up!"—to the new R-Truth, who is out in the crowd putting Little Jimmy down any chance I get, spilling his drinks, and even throwing a soda in Big Jimmy's face when I get the chance. In my mind, I don't like Little Jimmy because Little Jimmy has never liked me. That's my attitude out there and I just go with it, but I have to give all the credit to Creative for how we reinvented R-Truth. Everything goes through Vince McMahon first, and when they gave me the chance to take my character in a new direction and even go out into the crowd and mix things up with the fans, it was awesome. It's such a rush, I love it.

And for me to go after Cena like I did, it was R-Truth letting everyone know that if you're going to pick a fight with somebody, you go after the biggest guy in the room. You don't get anywhere going after puppies. You need to go after the big dogs, and that's what they let me do.

This was my first main event, and the crowd was going crazy when I walked to the ring. I had so much emotion, so much adrenaline heading down the aisle, because here I was at the top of the chain for the biggest wrestling company on the planet. I had worked so hard for so many years to get here, and as I walked to the ring, that's all I could think about. I've accomplished a lot of things that a lot of other people have never been able to accomplish, and in that moment, I knew it was my time.

You know why? I believe in myself, and I've always believed in myself to the utmost, so to me, this was really just the beginning of R-Truth. To me, I worked so hard to get where I was, and this feud with John Cena was like a new beginning to me. This was where people really started to pay attention to me. And it's so awesome working with John. I love working with John. We have the chemistry down, he trusts me out there, and he makes me feel really comfortable. He wasn't out there acting like he was a bigger star or better than me. We went out there and worked the match and had fun.

The move I loved the most in this match is when he hooked me up for the Attitude Adjustment and I twisted out of it and hit him with the suplex stunner, which I call the Cold Shoulder. That was nice. And then I really liked how we did the end of the match. It was the perfect story-line of "What goes around, comes around." I was outside the ring and I got taken out by Little Jimmy. He threw a drink in my face, and while the drink somehow managed to be shockingly cold and refreshing all at the same time, it enabled John to finish me off from there. Little Jimmy got his due and helped beat me. But that's cool because, like I said, what goes around comes around.

What was great was the reaction from the boys in the back. I've made so many friends throughout my career, and it was really special to me that so many of them were there to see this moment. They were patting me on the back and telling me how proud of me they were. It feels good when you hear things like that from your peers. I had been through so much in my career, but right then I knew that this was something special.

18

ALEX RILEY

The Match: Alex Riley versus The Miz
Capitol Punishment

June 19, 2011
Verizon Center
Washington, D.C.

I was on Season Two of *NXT* as a WWE rookie, but I didn't win the show. Miz was my mentor on *NXT*, and after the season was over, he came to me and asked if I wanted to work with him. I thought it would be great and an amazing way to learn the business. This was my shot at being in the WWE, and in return, I would act as his apprentice. I appreciated the opportunity and everything Miz had given me, but there were a lot of times where I started to feel that I wanted to go on my own path. But at the same time, being with Miz really helped put me in a great position. All of a sudden I went from *NXT* to getting to work with Miz and guys like The Rock and Stone Cold and Roddy Piper and John Cena. Being a rookie in the business, it was an incredible jump from losing a reality show to being around the main event picture, and I owe that all to The Miz. I was extremely fortunate to have that opportunity.

But as things started going bad for Miz in the ring and he started to lose, he tried to use me as a scapegoat, and his goal on the show was to embarrass me on national TV. And what people might not realize is that when he was embarrassing me and I turned on him and started beating him down, there was a lot of real emotion there. We had been traveling together for almost a year, and as much as we did like and respect each other, there were other times where we did get on each other's nerves. We have almost a big brother–little brother type of relationship, and the truth is, I did want to go out on my own. I saw other people in WWE who got the opportunity from the start to be their own man, and I always wanted to do that. At some point, I wanted to walk my own path, and at the same time, I think Miz was getting a little frustrated because he thought he was carrying me. And at that point, maybe he was. His career allowed me a lot of opportunities that I wouldn't have gotten otherwise, at least not this early. I was shot into a *WrestleMania* storyline my first year, where it had taken him a long time to get there, and I think he might have felt that I didn't deserve it. And then, like I said, I had the feeling that I wanted to break away from this guy, and I think that had a lot to do with how our fights on *Raw* came off so well leading up to the match at *Capitol Punishment*.

It was just so real, because a lot of the things he said, he really believed, and when I snapped that first night on *Raw*, it was because of a lot of things that I really believed. When that moment was captured on live TV for the WWE Universe, what the fans saw was truly two best friends who had finally had enough and just went after each other. It culminated in that moment, and I think it will be one of the top moments on *Raw* in 2011. It was a really good night, and the crowd really ate it up. I think the fans responded due to the combination of him being hated for so long and how he's so good at pulling emotion out of the WWE Universe and making people dislike him, and the fact that people really wanted to see him get his butt kicked. It was 50 percent that and 50 percent me having enough. I wasn't leaving there until I was finished with him and he was left lying in the middle of the ring. It was good.

And then when *Capitol Punishment* rolled around, that was a moment I had been waiting for for a long time. It was made even more special because it was in Washington, D.C., my hometown, so a lot of my family and friends were there to see my first big match on a Pay-Per-View. Not only that, but this first match was against a former WWE Champion. From *NXT* to WWE, by no means did I walk in thinking I was going to take the place over. I know that it takes a long time to make an impact, but I was waiting for my moment where I could make that impact. Before the match started, I was very confident and I was ready to go. This was my chance to walk on my own and make my presence felt. I was very excited and very fortunate that I got to do it in front of my friends and family.

The high school that I went to is twenty-five minutes away from the Verizon Center, and a lot of my character to that point was built around the guy I was in high school. In *NXT*, I even wore the letterman jacket that was very similar to my high school's letterman jacket, so it was perfect. I couldn't have written a better start to a WWE career. The way it all worked out was just unbelievable, especially when it came to the end of this match. I hit Miz with a DDT and he didn't get up, so there I was standing in the ring with twenty thousand fans screaming, and I started my career 1–0 in Pay-Per-Views. I'll always remember that moment. You always remember your breakout moments, and the night I first split from Miz and then our match at *Capitol Punishment* are the two moments in my career that I'll never forget.

19

ZACK RYDER

The Match: Zack Ryder versus Primo
WWE Superstars

June 13, 2011
Nassau Veterans Memorial Coliseum
Uniondale, New York

I have an Internet following with this YouTube show I've been doing called "Z! True Long Island Story," so, this being my return to Long Island, it was like the whole place was waiting for me to come out. The fans reacted so loudly, I felt like I was Steve Austin for the night, it was that crazy. There were signs everywhere. My family was there, my friends were all in the audience, and it was just an unbelievable night for me. I went out wearing blue and orange, the color of the Islanders, and everything was just really cool.

The fans really made my night. When I first started my YouTube show, I really wasn't sure how long I could keep it up, but the videos have really ended up taking on a life of their own. The week before my match with Primo, I did this whole training montage on my show getting ready for Long Island. I was doing push-ups and drinking eggs, and I think everyone saw that and got hyped for my comeback. And at the time, I was a bad guy on TV, but when I grabbed the mic before the match and started talking, the people loved me. It was my night, and that night helped people in the back realize that the fans really do want to see Zack Ryder. I can be a player in WWE.

What I realized about this business is that there's only one person to blame if you don't succeed, and that's yourself. I didn't want to look back on my career with any regrets, so I said, "Hey, I gotta get my name out there, and what better way than social media?" Social media is everywhere, so I did my best to embrace it, and out of nowhere, someone like me—who wasn't really featured much on WWE television—is in *Sports Illustrated* and named one of the top 100 athletes on Twitter. I'm the only WWE Superstar on that list, so it has to open some eyes. And what's cool is how social media has really helped get not only my name, but my catchphrase known by a larger audience. Like the night of this match, the fans were going nuts and they started chanting, "Woo-woo-woo!" with me as I was saying it.

It's so funny to me when I hear the crowd chant "Woo-woo-woo!" along with me during my match because of how the phrase really started. It's something I came up with when I was with my buddies a few years ago. "Woo-woo-woo!" was a way to pick up a hot girl in a club. I don't know if it really worked, but when a hot girl would walk by, that's what we'd say. We thought it was funny. So when I needed a catchphrase and I needed something to stand out, I went back to what I thought was funny in my day-to-day life. "Woo-woo-woo!" Now everybody wants to be a broski.

Things like that never would've happened without my show. For so many years I had been a bad guy and I had been booed, then instantly that night, everyone in the building was cheering me on, chanting my name and saying my catchphrase with me. And to have my family and friends there to hear the people's reaction to every little thing I did and the atmosphere in the building just made everything feel even more special to me. Even though this was just a match on *WWE Superstars*, it felt like a main event, and I owe that to the fans. The fans got me on TV because they wanted to see me so bad, they wanted Zack Ryder merchandise, and this match was such an eye-opener to a lot of people about how passionate my fans can be. I think we stole the show from a crowd-reaction standpoint, so when I hit the Rough Ryder, the crowd screamed, "One-Two-Three!" It felt like a Hulk Hogan match—or, at least, it felt that way to me.

20

TRIPLE H

The Match: Triple H versus Shawn Michaels
SummerSlam

August 25, 2002
Nassau Veterans Memorial Coliseum
Uniondale, New York

Shawn had not wrestled for almost five years leading up to our match. He had been out with back surgery and basically retired from the business. Shawn and I had been very, very close for a lot of years, but it's no secret that Shawn had a lot of drug problems and issues in his life, so we had a falling-out. We were on good terms when he left, but we really stopped getting along after he came back a few times to be commissioner of the show. I hate to say he was screwing up, but he had a lot of problems going on at this time. The demons were really on him, and since I was the person closest to him, he tried to take his problems out on me, or blame me, and that got to the point where Shawn and I didn't talk for a long time.

But then Shawn cleaned himself up and he found religion and was saved, so to speak, and that was a big changing point in Shawn's life. He completely cleaned himself up, and literally right before this happened, we talked the day before his big epiphany, and at one point in time as we continued to talk and renew our friendship, Shawn said: "You know what, my kid is getting older and I would just love for him to see what I can do just one time. I can't do it full time, physically, I know that, and I'm not sure if I can even do it one time, but I know if I did, I could do it with you. You will protect me." Shawn trusted me. I think he felt that I was the only guy at that time who could do a match with him and he'd feel safe. There was the real fear that he could come out of this match crippled if things didn't go well, but we talked to Vince, we talked Vince into it, and we booked the match. This was only supposed to be a one-time thing. We were going to wrestle each other one time, that was it. He was going back into retirement. That was the plan, at least.

I was thrilled and touched and honored that he would choose me to wrestle in his first match back and that he had that much confidence in my ability in the ring, but there was a lot of pressure going into this match. I'd be bringing one of the greatest ever back into the ring, and it felt like his physical well-being was in my hands. As much as Shawn wanted to have a great match, I think there's a part of him that would have been okay with it if he didn't have a great match. He had been off for five years, so it was understandable. He would just go back home and go back to doing what he was doing . . . no big deal. He was a little more accepting of that, but not me. That wasn't an option for me. I've always put more pressure on myself when I'm doing something for someone else than when I'm doing it for me. I've never felt the pressure nearly as much when I'm winning the title than when I'm losing it to somebody else. If I was winning, whatever. To me, the pressure comes when I'm working Batista at *WrestleMania* and I'm trying to make this win so good for him; it becomes one of those moments people remember. And it's the same thing here with Shawn. If this was going to be his last match, I just wanted to make it so good for him. But the funny thing is, Shawn and I decided that we were going to work and we talked about it with

Vince, but we never really spoke about the match again after the initial pitch. We knew we were going to do it at *Summer-Slam* and that was it. Shawn didn't even want to come to the building the day of the match because he didn't want to get distracted, so he called me and I went over to his hotel. I was there for maybe an hour at the most, and we hardly even spoke about the match, we were just bullshitting a little bit.

At this point in time, remember, we still weren't the best of friends. We were just at the point of patching things up. We were getting there. So we just kind of talked and bullshitted about things. It was weird, though, because we didn't talk about how the match would go down because we really didn't know what to expect. We really didn't know what Shawn would even have. At one point, he even said, "I really don't know what I can even give you." So I was like, "We'll know once we get in there and then we'll figure it out." And that's just how we left it. We decided to just wing it. We were just going to go off of emotion and go off of the crowd. There's hardly anybody in the business right now who can do that. I can count them on one hand. And not to toot our own horns, but I don't think there were that many guys who could do it back then either.

But it's not like we knew our match was going to be some classic. When you talk to Shawn, you'll know he is the least self-confident guy out there, unless you're talking to me. We all live the same thing. You go out on TV and tell everyone in the world that you're the greatest thing, that you're the best. And then you stand in front of the curtain before your music hits and you doubt everything you've ever said and everything that's ever been said about you. Or, vice versa, you believe every rotten thing that's ever been said about you and you go out there and try to prove them wrong. Shawn has always been that way, and that night, more so than any night in his career, he just didn't believe in himself.

And because of that, we really didn't know what to expect once we got out there. Nobody did. We didn't go out there with a plan, we just went and did it, and I remember it being very emotional. Shawn was very emotional that night. He was scared and his wife was scared, and I remember seeing all of his family hugging him backstage before the match, and his mom came to me with tears in her eyes and she could hardly speak. I just told her, "I will not let anything happen to your boy. You have nothing to worry about. He will not get hurt. He'll be fine." She just said, "Thank you," and she started to cry and walked away. It was a ton of pressure, to say the least. I was nervous and scared to death. For me, I wanted to go out there and have Shawn's one final match and show people what he could still do. If this really was the last time he was going to do this, I wanted it to be the best he'd ever had. At the same time, I didn't want him hurt in any way, shape, or form. Shawn is like a brother to me, and even though we weren't the best of friends and we had our falling-out, I didn't want him to get hurt or injured out there. So it was intense and really emotional going into it, and when we finally got inside the ring, I'll never forget, we just started fighting. We were only a minute or two into the match, and in my mind I was like, "Jesus Christ, he has not lost a step. This guy is still as good as he was when I wrestled him six years ago." There's a timing in our business, there's a rhythm to it, and when you haven't done it for even a brief period of time, they call it ring rust. And it's so true, because when you don't wrestle for a while, that timing is just not there. You think you're doing everything right, but you're not, and it's tough to deal with when you're the other guy.

But in this match, there was no ring rust. It was like Shawn had wrestled the day before and this was just another night. Shortly into the match, I said something to him like, "Hey dude, relax, this is going to be so easy." And we just went out there and did it. We beat the shit out of each other and he didn't get hurt. I think he was happy with the match—I know I was—and the biggest thing I was happy with was that on that night, I think we gave the wrestling business back Shawn Michaels. It could've gone either way, but that night set the table for him to be back, and his return lasted almost eight years.

It was also the return of our friendship. Once we did the match at *SummerSlam* and Shawn came back later that year and decided he could do more, he and I started to travel together and we had become very close again. Once we were on the road, it was like family again. To me, I almost look at Shawn like my brother. We don't call each other every day and we don't talk all the time, but when we do talk, it's like no time has passed and we catch right up. There was a period of time where we didn't speak, but as soon as we were back where we were traveling together and in the same environment, there we were again, best friends. It didn't matter if we were working against each other or working together as DX, we just have this chemistry together, and I truly do feel like he's my brother. That's why this match was so emotional for me and why it means so much to me on so many different levels.

21

WILLIAM REGAL

The Match: William Regal versus Chris Jericho
WWE *Backlash*

April 29, 2001
Allstate Arena
Rosemont, Illinois

I fought Chris Jericho in this match where we had to abide by the Duchess of Queensbury Rules, but the thing is, nobody was told of the rules beforehand, so every time it looked like Jericho had won the match, he didn't, and the crowd just kept getting angrier and angrier. What would happen is, Chris would do something that should've won the match. But then the Duchess would ring the bell, and Howard Finkel would explain to the crowd some obscure rule—like the time limit had just expired in round one, or the fact that Chris could not win by submission after he had just made me tap out . . . So the match would continue, with Jericho throwing a tantrum and getting the crowd all worked up about how unfair this all was.

We had the Duchess there at ringside, and she was dressed in this ridiculous garb. Then, of course, me being me, we did this spot where I flew over the top rope and landed with my head right in her lap. I came up from there and pulled out one of my ridiculous old faces, where it looks like I've been served an obscene amount of lemons. I looked at Jericho with this face and he just burst out laughing. He couldn't hold it in. The whole audience was laughing at this point, and when you see a picture of that moment or watch it on video, it's probably the best facial expression I've ever made during a match. I had been besmirched. Jericho then rolled the Duchess into the ring, but when he was distracted, I hit him with a chair and pinned him thanks to the Duchess's rules that made the match no-disqualification. But to me, this match is all about that one moment and my reaction to landing in the Duchess's lap. This was definitely not the best match I've ever been in, but it definitely had my favorite moment.

The story behind the match was also unique. It started with Jericho urinating in my tea when I was the commissioner, and then naturally things built up from there, as they tend to do when someone urinates in your tea. As the commissioner, I was abusing my power and doing anything in my ability to get under his skin after the tea incident, and then before you knew it, I was besmirched.

It's always great working with someone like Jericho because we're both really well schooled in what we do. We've both wrestled all around the world and we're both able to do different styles of matches, and that's something rare today. He's got that flair for entertainment that I've got, where we're both willing to go in any direction to entertain the crowd. The way people react to what you're doing in the ring isn't always the way you might think going in, so you need to be able to adapt. Sometimes you need to go serious, sometimes you need to give each other a good slap to get a reaction, and Jericho is very accommodating to work with, as he's always willing and able to go that extra mile in order to make the crowd react. Other performers out in the ring aren't like that anymore. We're a dying breed, so that's why it's always special to get in there with a guy like Jericho and see what happens—even if it ends up with my face in the lap of a Duchess.

22

JACK SWAGGER

The Match: Jack Swagger versus Christian
WWE *Backlash*

April 26, 2009
Dunkin' Donuts Center
Providence, Rhode Island

From winning Money in the Bank at *WrestleMania* to wrestling for the ECW Championship, I've had some great moments so far in my career. But I think my favorite match is my match at *Backlash* against Christian. The thing about working with Christian is that he's a great teacher out in the ring, and he taught me a lot during our matches for the ECW title. We both really brought our A-game to *Backlash* and put on a match I'll never forget.

This is back when Christian first returned to WWE after being out on hiatus and I was only a few months into my ECW title reign. I was thinking I would be the ECW Champion for the rest of the year at this point, but then Christian came out of nowhere, and day one, he was back to being a major player. Our first match together, he beat me, and to be honest, that really bothered me and it stuck with me as I trained. Then we ended up going on tour, and every week, we were just getting better and better chemistry out there and we were going after it. Then we did our match at *Backlash*, and everything just peaked at that moment.

My favorite spot was when I gorilla pressed him outside of the ring. But I didn't just throw him over the ropes; I threw him outside of the corner of the ring over the top of the ring post. From there, we went into this ending that had a whole string of false finishes, and the crowd was eating everything up and was really kept on the edge of their seats. He hit me with a tornado DDT and everybody thought it was over, but I kicked out, then he went into the sunset flip out of a springboard from the corner. He does that a lot now, but I take credit for it because he started it with me. Anyway, I remember when he finally hit the one-two-three after the Killswitch, the crowd erupted bigger than anything I'd heard in one of my matches before. It was awesome how loud it got.

As a younger performer, I hadn't been in many big situations at that time, and I'd never heard the crowd go that big. But the crowd really lets you know where to go with the match; and when you're with a veteran like Christian or with Undertaker, they know where to take the match because they can feel the crowd's reaction. They know what to do because they've been there. When you're in the ring with someone like Christian, if you want to, you can learn so much from them, and I feel like I really did in terms of timing and going into false finishes and selling and when it's time to get up and go. I learned so many little things during my run with Christian, and any great wrestler will tell you, it's the little things that make good matches great matches.

And when you're out there, as a performer, you know when things are going good or when things are going bad, but I think you can't really tell if a match is great until you go back and watch it. The greatest compliment in our business is when you go backstage and you get compliments from your co-workers and your bosses and producers. That's when you know you hit one out of the park.

I was very fortunate early in my career to work with Christian and Finlay and Tommy Dreamer. They took care of me in the ring and really taught me a lot about how to put on great matches. They've all done wonders for me in my career and put me on the right path to where I am today.

23

RICKY "THE DRAGON" STEAMBOAT

The Match: Ricky "The Dragon" Steamboat versus Randy "Macho Man" Savage
WrestleMania III

March 29, 1987
Pontiac Silverdome
Pontiac, Michigan

At the time it happened, my match against Randy Savage at *WrestleMania III* was not my favorite match. In fact, it probably took ten years for this match to really sink in for me. When we put the match together, we knew we had a lot going for us: One, the match was taking place at *WrestleMania*. And two, Hulk Hogan and Andre the Giant were the headliners of the event, and with the numbers we were hearing about the Pay-Per-View as well as the tickets being sold at the Silverdome, we both understood that there were going to be a whole lot of people watching this show, and possibly a record-breaking attendance. We had known for a while that Andre had a bad back and that Hogan would be limited with what he was going to be able to do with the big guy. That's not any fault to either one of them; it's just the wear and tear of your body over time, and especially to Andre being as big as he was, it was particularly hard on him. And I think the moment for that match was Hogan being able to pick up the five-hundred-pound guy and slam him. That being said, we were constantly thinking about the difference between what Randy and I could do out there compared to what was going to happen in the main event.

You see, in a typical A-B-C match at that time, the good

guy would have a moment where he looked really good in the match, and then it would be the bad guy's turn to have his moment in the match, to where he would have the babyface in a predicament, or maybe even several predicaments during his time of the match. Then when you got to the last part of the match, the good guy would typically have another good moment and that would be his comeback. It would be his turn to fight through the odds after being on the defensive during so much of the segment and he was just trying to survive while making the heel look good. Then it was on to the end of the match, where whoever was going to win would pull it out with one final move. Those were the A-B-Cs of matches in the 1970s and 1980s.

And that's what made the match Randy and I had so different. We had what we call a bunch of false finishes. I'm not sure of the exact number, but I think it was around twenty-one attempts for one guy to beat the other guy, and for the 1980s, in most matches, the attempts to pin would only be a handful. Then all of a sudden here comes this match where you have twenty-something attempts to win, following up on an angle that saw Randy come off the top rope on my throat with the bell and put me out for about two months leading up to *WrestleMania*. Here you had a guy looking for revenge in me, going up against a guy who would do anything to hold on to his championship in Savage.

And a lot of the credit for the buildup of this match has to go to Savage. Back then, wrestling was all about the bad guy doing something to the good guy and the fans waiting in anticipation for the good guy to come back and find redemption. And if memory serves me right, it was Randy's idea to use the ring bell, which had a piece of plywood bolted on to the back of it. He didn't just want to use a chair or some other object around the ring. But the most important part of selling this move was the fact that you can play it back from any angle and you couldn't dispute that he hit me. There weren't any gaps or holes in it. It looked like that thing nailed me right on the throat. We have an understanding out there that the things that we do are in very, very, very close quarters because of all the different TV angles. So when he hit me, it was solid, it was snug. I'm not going to deny that, but it's one of those situations you're hoping for and you just go for it.

After that angle aired, a lot of fan mail was sent to the office. I got everything from "I hope you recover soon," to "Can't wait for you to get back at Savage," to "God, I wonder if you'll ever be able to speak again, much less come back and wrestle." A lot of times, when my match against Savage is brought up, that moment of him hitting me with the ring bell is also brought up, so they are neck-and-neck about what people remember about me and our match at *WrestleMania*.

But when the match was over, I thought it was a good match; I guess I just didn't really realize the impact it had until years later. You wouldn't believe the number of wrestling fans who come up to me and talk about that match. Even after I retired, people would still come up to me and all they'd want to talk about was that match. But back then all I thought about was that we needed to put on a good match and take advantage of the situation, having the best match at *WrestleMania*. We did that, then it was recognized later on as Match of the Year, and it keeps being brought up throughout the years when they talk about the best matches of not only *WrestleMania*, but of all time. This match just keeps popping up.

Another thing that really made me start appreciating this match is that I started to notice the wrestling business changing throughout the years—and this is a big change—where the main events of Pay-Per-Views started to follow the criteria of what Randy and I did. It's no longer about the typical A-B-C match. Now you see a lot of attempts to win being made, and you even see that criteria in one of the greatest matches that I've ever seen, Shawn Michaels versus Undertaker at *WrestleMania XXV*. I don't know if what Randy and I did set the tone to help make that match one of those unforgettable moments, but I have a gut feeling because it was brought up so many times to me that they used our match as a base to take everybody on an up-and-down ride full of emotion throughout all of their false finishes. I don't know for sure, but I have a gut feeling, and my gut feeling has usually been right throughout the years when I watch guys perform.

But I have to say—maybe on the rebound, maybe I was the last one to appreciate it even though I was in the match, and even though I've had a ton of matches with Ric Flair that were great—that my match against Savage is now my favorite, and a lot of it has to do with the public recognition. It's probably my biggest contribution to this business, and a lot of it has to do with how everybody remembers all of the false finishes and how that went on to change the way we see wrestling matches today. It's the match I'll always be remembered for, and now it's my favorite too.

24

KANE

The Match: Kane versus Undertaker

WrestleMania XIV

March 29, 1998
FleetCenter
Boston, Massachusetts

Pete Rose could've been one of the best heels in wrestling if he wanted to. I remember how he walked out at *WrestleMania XIV* to be the guest ring announcer, but instead of announcing the match, Pete cut one of the best heel promos I've ever heard, and every person in that arena was booing him. The funniest line of the night is when he said: "I left some tickets for Bill Buckner at the box office, but he couldn't bend over to pick them up."

A few minutes later, here I come down to the ring—this is my first *WrestleMania*, and it was only a few months after Kane debuted in WWE—and I tombstone Pete Rose right there in the middle of the ring. This ended up becoming a tradition for a few *WrestleManias*, where I would tombstone Pete Rose, and it's one of the things fans still ask me about all the time. Here I was, I'm supposed to be this big bad guy, and for a minute, at least, I came out and got this enormous pop from all the Red Sox fans in the audience. It was pretty funny.

Then again, I guess they loved me until Undertaker came out. Once his entrance started, the people stopped cheering for Kane. But that's because WWE had done such a tremendous job of building the anticipation for this match. In fact, as far as the craft of storytelling goes, I think the Undertaker/Kane feud is one of the best storylines the WWE has ever done. For months, Paul Bearer had been talking about how Undertaker had this big secret: that he had this long-lost brother named Kane, but nobody had ever seen him. Then back in October of 1997, Undertaker and Shawn Michaels fought in the first ever Hell in a Cell match, and that's when I made my debut, attacking Undertaker and costing him the match. And what was great about this story is that Undertaker didn't want to fight his brother, Kane, for months and months and months; and the buildup was great, because the whole time it was Kane on the offensive and the fans just couldn't wait for Undertaker to snap and get his revenge. You knew something big was going to happen at *WrestleMania* when these two monsters collided.

This was back before Undertaker's Streak had become a huge deal. His record at that point was good, but it wasn't 19–0. So for me to have my first *WrestleMania* moment and to have Undertaker as my opponent was pretty awesome and something that was really special to me. And the thing is, up until this point, I had just been steamrolling everyone in my way, so I think this is one of the first times, if not *the* first time, in Undertaker's career that he was the underdog in a match. That had never happened before.

But what's great about Undertaker is how he manages to bring out the best in his opponents. When you're going up against him, you want to go out and do your best, and size-wise, we really match up well in the ring. I'm one of the few guys who match up physically with Undertaker in terms of size and athleticism, and you don't see that too often, and I think that really helped add to the spectacle of the storytelling that was going on. People really wanted to see what would happen when Undertaker finally decided he had had enough and wanted to get his hands on Kane. Something bad was about to happen to somebody out in that ring.

This was back when I was wearing the red-and-black mask, and I think there were a lot of people in the crowd back then who were uneasy any time I even made my way to the ring with all that fire. Like Jim Ross says, when my music played, everyone knew business was about to pick up. But I think that mask also added a lot to the character, and how scary he looked and acted. The mask helped elevate the story because Kane was so mysterious and nobody ever knew what he was thinking, and you couldn't have done that without the mask. I still look back at the mask and think about how cool it was. There's a lot of history and a lot of nostalgia when I look back at this period, as there are really two different Kanes: the Kane without the mask and the masked Kane. They're really two different guys, and this match and this storyline were just the beginning.

As for the *WrestleMania* match itself and the moment that sticks out most in my mind, it has to be when Undertaker did his dive to the outside of the ring and I sidestepped him and he went flying through a table. That's one of those moments where it just looked awesome, whether you're a fan or his opponent or, in my case, both. Another thing that stands out is the fact that it took three Tombstones to beat me. I don't think that had ever happened before, so it was a unique and brutal finish.

And to be honest, I was relieved the match went as well

as it did. There was a lot of pressure on me to deliver. They had built this whole storyline, this whole program that lasted over six months and involved one of WWE's top Superstars in Undertaker, so the match had to be good. I had to deliver in order to make Kane into something special. And while I think the match was good, I actually look back and wish I could do it over again because I think I could do it better. Now that I'm a seasoned performer, I watch the match over and wish I could do a few things differently. I'm still happy with it overall because it delivered what needed to be delivered, and that's part of the reason I've been with WWE for so long: because they know that I can deliver on a big stage like *WrestleMania*, and this match helped me prove it. This match is where Kane really got his start, and I have Undertaker—and, of course, Pete Rose—to thank.

25

REY MYSTERIO

**The Match: Rey Mysterio
versus Eddie Guerrero
WCW *Halloween Havoc***

October 26, 1997
The MGM Grand Garden Arena
Las Vegas, Nevada

I walked into the MGM Grand Garden Arena thinking this was going to be my last night ever wrestling under my mask. This was back when Eric Bischoff was screwing with me in WCW. He wanted to show that he was the boss. He wanted to let everyone know who had the power backstage, so he decided to forget about tradition. He decided to forget about my legacy. He told me my mask was coming off.

So in this match, Eddie had the cruiserweight championship at the time, and they made it a Mask versus Title match. I clearly remember walking up to Eddie and Eddie telling me, "Forget about everything, let's just go out there and tear up the house." But then right before we went out—and I'm talking about minutes before the match—I was told that they had changed their minds and I wasn't losing the mask. Not yet. They were saving that for another night. It was about two years later when the mask eventually came off, but from *Halloween Havoc* on, the word was already out that they wanted to unmask me, not knowing that there is a big history behind masked wrestlers, myself in particular. I started at age fourteen under the mask, carrying on not only the culture of the masked wrestler, but the legacy and the name of my uncle's career, and carrying on the name of Rey Mysterio. They wanted to take off my mask without thinking about the future ahead of me. I don't know if my career would've been different if I never lost my mask and then went to WWE without people knowing who Rey Mysterio really was. I can't go back in time now, but I do ask myself this question: Would my career have been any different if I never lost my mask in WCW?

But luckily, at least for this night, the mask stayed on, and like Eddie said, we tore up the house at *Halloween Havoc*. Our chemistry in the ring together was just amazing that night. That's the match where we realized we really had something special between us in the ring. I was able to do moves in the ring with Eddie that I've never been able to do with anybody else, that's how special our chemistry was. Even after all these years, there were moves in this match that I've never done again.

Go back and watch this match again and you'll see some amazing sequences. One of my favorites is when I went to do a suicide dive out onto the floor. It was a normal dive— hit the ropes, front flip over the top rope—but I overrotated a little bit and I landed in a powerbomb position on top of Eddie's shoulders. He caught me and then pulled me in and I gave him a Frankensteiner to the floor. Eddie had an incredible physique back then—this was probably the peak of his strength—and a move like this showed how strong he was. No matter how light I was at the time, this was something that was difficult to pull off.

Back then, I didn't do the 619 how I do it now, and it didn't even have a name in those days, but I came around to do my variation of the 619, and instead of connecting to his face, my legs wrapped around his neck. We did a complete 360, where my body came into the ring and then over the top rope in a variation of the head scissors, knocking Eddie all the way down to the floor.

The finish was also a fun moment to watch. It was a move called Splash Mountain that was similar to the Razor's Edge. Eddie was standing on the second turnbuckle, and he lifted me up from my armpits to where I was looking out into the crowd. But when he lifted me up, I turned it into a Frankensteiner for the one-two-three.

But to be honest, the biggest move of the night, and the most memorable sequence of the match, wasn't even the finish, and it's a move I've never seen duplicated in the same way again. It was a backflip DDT. I was lying on the mat, and Eddie grabbed me by the hands and launched me into the air to the point where I was able to land on the top rope. I jumped into a backflip, and somehow on my way down I hooked him into a DDT and we went down. It was crazy. That was one of those moves that wasn't even called. We never intended to do something like that when we were talking about the match backstage. It was just something that happened in the moment of action. I don't remember what I was trying to do, but I landed in a DDT position and just never let go when my arm wrapped around his head. We just went with the flow. I remember landing and we both just looked at each other and were like, "What the fuck was that! That was awesome!" We were just both really excited that something was invented that night.

Another reason this match stands out to me is that the outfit I wore that day had a lot of meaning for me. It was custom-made from one of my designers in Japan, and in the back of the outfit, he had put the name of my son, Dominik, who was born that year. His name was airbrushed in such a way where you really had to look hard at the outfit to catch it, but just knowing his name was there meant a lot to me because that was such an important year in my life thanks to my son's birth. The whole outfit was really cool, though, as it was purple and black and based on the superhero movie *The Phantom*. I had done previous superhero outfits in ECW, like Superman and Batman, but this Phantom one really stands out. I actually still have the outfit with me in a frame, and it continues to hold a lot of meaning to me every time I look at it. It will always have meaning and will never die down. This is one of those trophies that I will pass down to my children, and they will pass it down to their children and their children's children one day. To be able to pass this on to my grandchildren one day, if I'm so lucky, will hold special meaning as I talk about this match and this special day in my life as an entertainer.

26

ALBERTO DEL RIO

The Match: Alberto Del Rio (Dos Caras Jr.) and Dos Caras versus El Azteca and Hayabusa

October 11, 2000

Shimonoseki, Japan

My favorite match is my first match, because I had the chance to team up with my father, the legendary Dos Caras. I was always a big fan of my father. As a little kid, I always dreamed of being like my dad. So the fact that I did that in Japan in my first match with my father in a sold-out arena was just amazing. I fulfilled my childhood dream that night. I was only twenty-two years old and my father was fifty-five, and we were going up against two Japanese wrestlers, El Azteca and Hayabusa.

I was so nervous because everybody was there to see me wrestle for the first time. All of the media were there from Japan, some media showed up from Mexico, and in the end, the match was actually really good. Of course, we were the winners of that match, and that was the start of my career.

My father had been this superstar in Japan and Mexico, so when they knew I was ready to be a pro, they called to tell me that they really wanted me to have my first match in Japan. They had a lot of sponsors and a lot of money riding on my debut, and they picked those guys because Hayabusa knew how to wrestle in the Mexican style and El Azteca was always a big fan of my father, so that's how the four of us ended up in the ring together. And it was incredible. Like I said, it was my childhood dream come true,

177

but I was so nervous. My skin might be brown, but that night I was white I was so scared. I was out there breathing heavy, and my father just kept telling me, "Relax, you're going to be okay. You're a great performer. You're going to do great." The first two minutes were the most difficult, but after that, everything was fine. And what's cool is that my father always used the cross-body as his finish in Japan, so I did it in my first match and the crowd went crazy, because to them it was like watching my father when he was younger. And of course, I like to kick a lot, so I used all of my kicks that you see today, like my step-up kick. I've been doing the same moves since I started, only now I'm using more of the American style, but the moves are basically the same.

Throughout the years leading up to this match, my dad told me so many things to help me become a better wrestler. In fact, he's still telling me things. And when you're hearing this advice from a legend like my father, these are the little things that have really helped elevate me in my career. I think his advice and the things he has told me throughout the years is one of the reasons I've been so successful in WWE. I know this business. And one of the things I always tell my friends, and the thing I tell anybody who wants to get into this business, is the same thing my father told me: Stand in front of the mirror and talk to yourself. Ask yourself what you need to do in order to be a superstar. Everybody will try to lie to you, but you will never lie to yourself. I looked in that mirror all the time, and I still do. When I was trying out for the Mexican national team and I was trying to be the best wrestler in my country, that's what I would do. I would ask myself what

I needed to do to be the best, and then I would go do it. I would look in the mirror and say: "You need to train more, you need to run more, you need to work more on this and that." Then I did the same when I turned pro and I still do it now in WWE. I look in that mirror and ask: "What do you need to do to be WWE champion? What do you need to do to get past 'champion' and become a 'legend'?"

And I still go back and watch this match. I'm so happy that I got the chance to work in Japan and Mexico before I debuted in WWE. That's another reason why I think I've been so successful. I've been able to wrestle all around the world and learn so many different things, and I think that's made me more complete. I used to wrestle under a mask in Mexico, and the way they work is just so completely different than what WWE does. In WWE, there's a reason for everything we do in the ring. There's logic behind every move. Whether it's a dropkick or a punch, there's a reason for everything. *Lucha Libre* style is beautiful, but in *Lucha Libre*, we just do things because it looks spectacular, but there's no logic. In WWE, we take those same moves, but we give them meaning, and that gives every move so much more impact. And I always say this: WWE is the Hollywood of sports entertainment. Everything is so much bigger. I'm out walking red carpets. I'm in a video game, I have an action figure. It's been an amazing ride so far, and when I look back, I look at my first match to think about how it all started. I never could've imagined that one day I'd be riding to the ring in a Bentley.

Acknowledgments

I'd like to thank all of the WWE Superstars past and present who spent so much of their downtime (and believe me, they don't get much downtime) talking to me about their favorite matches. As a wrestling fan since grammar school, you could only imagine what it was like to sit down with the likes of Ricky Steamboat, Roddy Piper, and "The American Dream" Dusty Rhodes. You all entertained and continue to entertain me for hours on end, and getting to hear these stories from the men who lived them was an awesome experience I'll never forget. Besides, how can I ever get the image of Randy Orton lying down in his living room on a thumbtack out of my head?

Special thanks to Dean Miller, Paul Levesque, Mark Carrano, Mike Archer, Ann Russo, and the entire WWE crew for helping arrange the interviews. And thanks to Emilia Pisani for her patience throughout the editorial process.

I'd also like to thank my kids, Brenden and Caroline, who spent the summer cracking me up as only they can, saying things like, "Dad, The Miz is on the phone for you . . . *Awesome!*"

Last, but certainly not least, I'd like to thank my wife, Nicole, for her love, understanding, and mad barbecue skills throughout the writing of this book. I couldn't have done it without you (or J.R.'s beef jerky).

About the Author

Jon Robinson writes "The Gamer" column for ESPN.com and *ESPN The Magazine* and is currently working on his first novel (although he'd rather be wrestling inside a steel cage).